He Loved Me, He Loves Me Not

A GUIDE TO FUDGE, FURY, FREE TIME, AND LIFE BEYOND THE BREAKUP

Written by Lynn Harris

Illustrated by Chris Kalb

AVON BOOKS NEW YORK

HE LOVED ME, HE LOVES ME NOT is an original publication of Avon Books. This work has never before appeared in book form.

AVON BOOKS
A division of
The Hearst Corporation
1350 Avenue of the Americas
New York, New York 10019

Text copyright © 1996 by Lynn Harris
Front cover and interior illustrations copyright © 1996 by Chris Kalb
Book design by Chris Kalb
Published by arrangement with the author
Library of Congress Catalog Card Number: 95-49280
ISBN: 0-380-78443-2

Library of Congress Cataloging in Publication Data:

Harris, Lynn.
    He loved me, he loves me not / Lynn Harris : illustrated by Chris Kalb.
        p.   cm.
Includes index.
1. Single women—Psychology—Miscellanea.   2. Separation (Psychology)—Miscellanea.   3. Dating (Social customs)—Miscellanea.   4. Man-woman relationships—Miscellanea.   I. Kalb, Chris.   II. Title.
HQ800.2.H37   1996   95-49280
646.7'7—dc20   CIP

First Avon Books Trade Printing: June 1996

AVON TRADEMARK REG. U.S. PAT. OFF. AND IN OTHER COUNTRIES, MARCA REGISTRADA, HECHO EN U.S.A.

Printed in the U.S.A.

QP 10 9 8 7 6 5 4 3 2 1

To my friends with all my love,
and to my ex-boyfriends with all due respect.

– Lynn

To Sonya, who didn't break up with me,
no matter how fun Lynn made it sound.

– Chris

ACKNOWLEDGMENTS

Thanks to:

Mom and Dad, for your omniscience, support, editing, sacrifices, and patience. And the clothing allowance.

Chris. You are a genius and a delight to work and live with. Thank God we've never dated.

Rita Rosenkranz, devoted agent, for your wisdom and friendship.

Stephen S. Power, our man at Avon. Our book couldn't have been in cooler, smarter, funnier hands.

Juliet Siler. At least we'll always have each other.

Brian Frazer, without whom this book—and the world— would be considerably less funny.

Larry Berger (see photos, pp. 53, 119, and 139). With ex-boyfriends/co-authors like you, who needs friends?

Jason Jacobs. With housemates like you, who needs boyfriends?

Aaron Foeste, for your superior coaching in hockey and humor, life and love.

The Brooklyn Blades women's ice hockey team, where I learned that hockey means never having to say you're sorry.

Jennifer Berman, Marjorie Clapprood, Sarah Dunn, Cynthia Heimel, Nicole Hollander, Patricia Ireland, Fran Leibowitz, Joanna Lumley, Jennifer Saunders, Dale Spender, Lily Tomlin, Jane Wagner, and Dan Zevin, for your hilarity and inspiration.

The women of Something Extra. Married or single, we'll always be speed bumps on the road of love.

The Greater Boston chapter of the National Organization for Women. I miss you guys. No one beeps me anymore.

The New England Confectionery Company (NECCO), for the off-season shipment of candy hearts. You make Cambridge smell good.

Landmark Education Corporation, for the meaning and power of "by when?"

And thanks also to all the other folks who shared breakup lore: Jenny Lyn Bader, Joy Bines, Judy Bornstein, Melissa Burkhart, Kris DeForest, Gavin Edwards, Amelia Eisch, Mike Gerber, Kira Gould, Ben Greenman, Liza Goitein, Kate Guiney, Rob Healy, Marjorie Ingall, Amy Keyishian, Dana Kirchman, Colin Lingle, Aaron Naparstek, Emily Abedon, Sam Pratt, Joe Savastano, Shirley Sims, Mark Smuckler, Cynthia Tolley, Estelle Weyl, Ken Wood, Sonya Wysocki, Christina Zwart.

CONTENTS

Men Are Pigs-In-A-Blanket

CHAPTER

2

"I NEVER REALIZED HOW MUCH I ENJOY SPENDING TIME ALONE"
(BREAKUP MYTH #5)

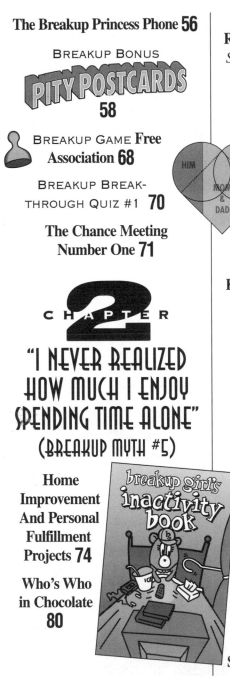

breakup girl's inactivity book

SEE YA

Been THERE, done HIM

C H A P T E R **5**

A BREAKUP ALMANAC

ACTUALLY, IT'S PRONOUNCED "PAY-TRONIZING"

INTRODUCTION

Smarting from a recent breakup?

You want more than anything to feel better, forgive, and move on.

Not.

What you *really* want is to wallow in your misery, wreak shrewd revenge—and never let them see you sweat. Breakup Girl will show you how.

For starters, you must memorize and recite The Breakup Creed:

Feel better, schmeel better.

It's only natural. You and I know from experience what psychologists have emerged from their offices to pronounce: that the trauma of breakup is analogous to that of grief over the death of a loved one. "Griefe," in fact—and I am not making this up—numbered among the top seven causes of death in London in 1657 (falling between "Hang'd and made away 'emselves" and "Found Dead in the Streets, etc.").

But check this out, [ex]girlfriend: we can look to the Huli people of Papua, New Guinea, for a safe and satisfying way to feel the pain. Apparently, Huli widows have a lower mortality rate than Huli widowers. How come? Anthropologists credit the tribe's therapeutic women-only tradition of spending at least one night—and up to several weeks—in a public "crying house" (*duguanda*), lamenting the loss and condemning the deceased for his poor timing.

More than three centuries later on the oppposite end of the earth, breakups continue to influence population trends. Here in the U.S., we have seen the emergence of a demographic group I'll call "Generation *Ex*." Baffling retro-styles and recycled music festivals notwithstanding, "free love" is over; marriage is back "in." People in their twenties, thirties, and even beyond now scrutinize their relationships more fiercely than ever—that is, under the harsh light of that single naked bulb, The M-Word. At this stage, the tingly little question "Can I see us spending breakfast together?" gives way to the far more brutal "Can I see us spending *THE REST OF OUR LIVES* together?" And when the answer is "no" (for at least 50% of the couple), it's the beginning of the end.

With so much at stake, these breakups tend to have excruciating effects and substantial ramifications (more so than, say, the time when Nicky Wadsworth dumped me for Katie Osborne at the Beach Dance on May 5, 1981). If only it were still as simple as sending a "Dear John" note in history class, moping for the duration of study hall, and writing new initials in the hearts on your notebook by geometry. But *no*: your skis are in his basement, your mutual friends are pawns in a turf war, his family and hometown are grieving, and all the faces in the *New York Times* wedding pages are laughing at you. *This* is the slice of life captured here in *He Loved Me, He Loves Me Not*.

Whether you're the dumper or the dumpee, Breakup Girl knows what you're going through. Breakups are prime territory for mixed feelings ("I am such a jerk for dumping that jerk!" "I never want to see you again … unless you're wearing those jeans."), so there's plenty of common ground and emotional overlap between the two parties. No matter what camp you're in—or even if the decision was bilateral—you're likely to plow through loneliness, guilt, resentment, second-thoughts, if-onlys...and at least teensy-weensy glimmers of relief and freedom. These are the universal feelings that Breakup Girl understands, addresses—and indulges.

Psychologists have also divided the grieving process into stages, and *He Loved Me, He Loves Me Not* has a chapter for each:

Shock	Zero: The Bomb
Awareness of Loss	One: The Fallout
Withdrawal	Two: "I Never Realized How Much I Enjoy Spending Time Alone" (Breakup Myth #5)
Healing	Three: Renewing Your Commitment to Personal Hygiene and Reentering Society
Renewal	Four: Beyond the Rebound—Moving On
Learning	Five: A Breakup Almanac

"Breakup Breakthrough" quizzes after each phase will help you track your progress. By the time you're done, you may really be ready to move on—or, at least, to New Guinea.

But unless you've boondoggled enough frequent-flier miles to get yourself to the South Pacific, consider this book your Beach Dance—I mean, your "duguanda."

Except in *this* duguanda, you can also laugh.

[signature]

Lynn Harris
Breakup Girl
Brooklyn, New York
1996

NOT SO LONG AGO, IN A TOWN NOT UNLIKE YOUR OWN...

THERE LIVED, AND LOVED, A GIRL NAMED LYNN

CHAPTER ZERO:
THE BOMB

*The impact of that
deadly heart-seeking missile
will be felt far and wide,
no matter who
pressed the button.*

Did I Do the Right Thing?

Breakup Girl knows perfectly well that breakups can be rough on dump*ee* and dump*er* alike. Sure, dumpees have to deal with rejection, loneliness, and helplessness that they certainly didn't ask for (well, maybe some did). But dumpers have to deal with the responsibility of inflicting all that on someone they were once gaga about, and who still does make them feel rather secure, loved, warm, fuzzy, and lustful.

That's a tough thing to do, a tough decision to make—especially if the breakup is in the realm of an impossible-to-explain gut feeling that "this just isn't working" (as opposed to "I'm leaving you because you embezzled money from my parents for a trip to Cozumel with one of your wood-shop students"). Those gut feelings can be so darned hazy. *Will I ever get over the guilt? If I'm so sure I wanted to end it, how come I still doodle his name in my food? Is it the relationship that's making me uncomfortable, or will I wake up tomorrow and realize that I just had something in my eye?*

Keep in mind that Breakup Girl does not endorse breakups for breakups' sake—those are hasty, nasty little impulses attributable to moon phases, mood swings, mood rings, and such. Breakup Girl does, however, encourage swift—yet sensible—action on breakups waiting (or *begging*) to happen. With "goodbye" out of the way, you can say "hello" to (a) the rest of your life, and (b) the rest of this book.

That said, check your motivations against this chart to see if your breakup is a hasty move—or Hallelujah material.

NOT A GOOD ENOUGH REASON

A GOOD ENOUGH REASON

he has an annoying laugh	he laughs when you're annoyed
he always has a bad mustache	he always has a Kool-Aid mustache
he misspelled your name on your Valentine (e.g. "Kelli" instead of "Kelly")	the Valentine really was for "Kelli"
your plants died in his care while you were away	you were away for only two days; they were all cacti
he dented your parents' car	he told them you did it
he called collect from Prague	he called collect from prison
he can't spell "hors d'oeuvres"	free Happy Hour hors d'oeuvres are his idea of taking you out for dinner
he taped over your copy of *Dirty Dancing*	he called his parents first for assistance with VCR operation
he read your diary	he corrected the grammar in your diary
he maintains a modest porn movie collection	he composed the musical score
his name didn't come up the last time you played that folded paper fortune-telling game	he wants you to meet his Psychic Friends
he doesn't like cookie dough	he doesn't like Jodie Foster
he won't hold your hand in public	he won't hold your hand in private
he moves around a lot in his sleep	he moved without telling you

DOIN' THE DEED

Breakup Technique

So by now you should have a clear sense of what you need to do. It's either:

a) get that thing out of your eye (see above), or

b) get that thing out of your life.

If (b) is the choice for you, welcome to The Hard Part, especially if the chap in question fits the "warm and fuzzy" description above rather than the "Cozumel caper" profile.

Some highly complex psychological and motivational—that is, *lack of* motivational—issues are about to come into play for you. But what it all boils down to in layperson's terms is that you *really would* break up...but you just don't *want* to. Indeed, the three most effective ways to forestall the pain and yuck of a breakup are, in ascending order:

❶ Resolve to break up as soon as you perform the seasonal rotation of your shoe tree.

❷ Resolve to break up as soon as all of your photographs from high school to present, including negatives, are ordered, labeled, and placed in albums. And you have made copies for everyone you've promised them to.

❸ Resolve to break up as soon as you figure out *how* to do the deed.

ENOLA, WHAT ARE YOU TRYING TO SAY?

Number Three (3) is where you're really going to get stuck. All of the variables boggle the mind. Oh, how you wish you could simply tell Susie to tell Bobby to tell Jane to write Scotty a note—*but don't say she heard anything from me!*—before homeroom.

But there's so much more to it than that. Should it be quick and dirty? Should you cushion the blow? (Reminder: **staying**

together does not count as a method of *cushioning the blow*.) How much of an explanation do you owe him? How much money do you owe him?

If you think for even an instant that there's only one right way to do this, you're right: *do it right away.* The more the question festers, the more confused you'll get, and the sooner you'll find yourself launching phase one of The Photo Project.

Phase One: Psyching Yourself Up

1. Notice his funny eating habits. Decide what type of food is most likely to cause them, and serve him lots of that.

2. Notice that your married friends never, ever use the word "I" unprefaced by, say, "Andrew and—"

3. Notice that your single friends, both of them —*oh, skip it*

4. Remember that when you get your tonsils removed, you get to eat ice cream. Notice an analogy.

5. Notice that you're already reading this book.

Phase Two: Location, Location, Location

Don't waste a lot of time on this one. Just employ common sense and common decency. You will thus, obviously, avoid islands, moving vehicles, any place you'll need a ride home from, and any sort of public ceremony. Any public place at all, in fact, will just not do. You may wish to take him out for a nice dinner in order to cushion the blow, but if you take him by surprise, you may then also need to move swiftly enough to cushion the blow of his forehead against the fajita skillet.

Phase Three: **Saying It**

This is the easy part, because he will not hear you.

WHAT YOU SAY: You are a wonderful boyfriend, but I feel like it's time for me to move on.
WHAT HE HEARS: You are a wonderful boyfriend.

WHAT YOU SAY: I can't live like this anymore.
WHAT HE HEARS: I can't lift this; will you help me get it off the floor?

WHAT YOU SAY: This may come as a shock to you, but I'm starting to feel like this thing is pretty much over.
WHAT HE SAYS: Yeah, I've sort of been feeling that way, too.
WHAT YOU SAY: *I said, this may come as a shock to you, but I'm starting to feel like this thing is pretty much over.* (God, he never listens.)

Phase Four: **How to Leave Things**

This is the hardest part. If you made a prudent choice in Phase Two, you will at least not be stuck waiting together for the once-daily ferry to the mainland. But no matter where you are, this is the beginning of the end. It's the *"now what?"* that hits you like hailstones. Prepare to be divebombed by questions like:

- So are we still friends?
- Do we call just to check in? How often?
- What am I going to do with those concert tickets?
- How am I supposed to get through the next ten minutes?
- How long before we wind up back in bed together against our better judgment?

Answer key:

- *Maybe eventually.*
- *Maybe eventually. We'll see how we feel.*
- *Won't your sister just have taken the PSATs? She'll need a treat.*
- *You will.*

- *Depends on the ferry schedule.*

**OTHER THAN THAT, YOU'RE ON YOUR OWN.
LITERALLY.**

Escape Routes Less Taken

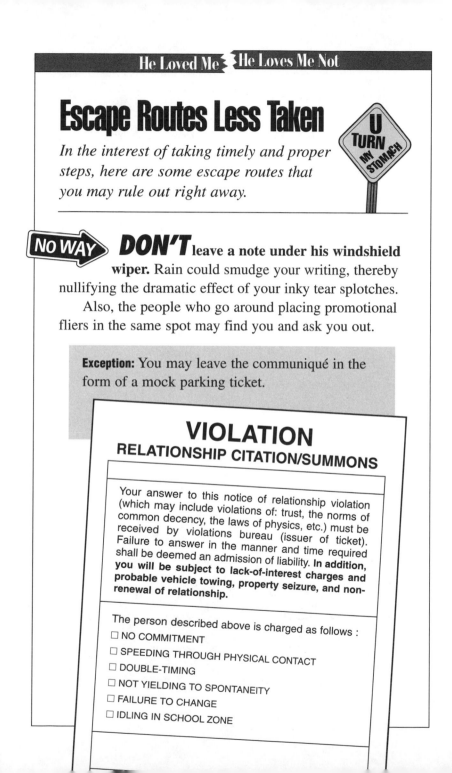

In the interest of taking timely and proper steps, here are some escape routes that you may rule out right away.

NO WAY ▶ ***DON'T*** **leave a note under his windshield wiper.** Rain could smudge your writing, thereby nullifying the dramatic effect of your inky tear splotches.

Also, the people who go around placing promotional fliers in the same spot may find you and ask you out.

> **Exception:** You may leave the communiqué in the form of a mock parking ticket.

VIOLATION
RELATIONSHIP CITATION/SUMMONS

Your answer to this notice of relationship violation (which may include violations of: trust, the norms of common decency, the laws of physics, etc.) must be received by violations bureau (issuer of ticket). Failure to answer in the manner and time required shall be deemed an admission of liability. **In addition, you will be subject to lack-of-interest charges and probable vehicle towing, property seizure, and non-renewal of relationship.**

The person described above is charged as follows :
☐ NO COMMITMENT
☐ SPEEDING THROUGH PHYSICAL CONTACT
☐ DOUBLE-TIMING
☐ NOT YIELDING TO SPONTANEITY
☐ FAILURE TO CHANGE
☐ IDLING IN SCHOOL ZONE

DON'T do it on-line. He may think it's some computer hacker's idea of a joke.

GET LOST

DON'T ask your doorman to do it for you.

HIT THE ROAD

The doorman might get faces mixed up and, thinking he's doing you a favor, mistakenly turn away other male suitors.

ESCAPE ROUTES LESS TRAVELLED

DON'T leave a message on his machine. The recording could be used in a court of law. Also, his constant rewinding and relistening could strain the county power supply.

GO AWAY

SO Long

ESCAPE ROUTES LESS TRAVELLED

DON'T do it **on a great-hair day.** It's harder to say goodbye— for both of you.

DON'T have your message posted on **the jumbo scoreboard of his favorite team.** It's too cruel, especially if he's a New Jersey Nets fan.

YOU LOSE

TAKE A HIKE

A GUIDE TO FUDGE, FURY, FREE TIME, AND LIFE BEYOND THE BREAKUP

He Loved Me, He Loves Me Not

LYNN HARRIS
ILLUSTRATED BY CHRIS KALB

DON'T present him **with a copy of this book,** highlighted. You're going to need it.

SCOOT

◆ RATE HIS RATIONALE ◆

Why he Dumped You

(And Why He May Very Well Have Done You A Favor)

So compared to dump*ing*, *being* dumped is a piece of cake.

Yep, a piece of cake topped with mocha-mayonnaise frosting, thumbtacks, and a big, huge brussels-sprout rose. And your ability to digest all that is going to have a lot to do with how and why he served it up.

OH, WELL

I want a change

I'm afraid to commit

I just can't deal with the long distance

I'm ready to move on

I'm joining the Peace Corps

This just isn't working out

We just aren't the right match

FROM HELL

I want that exchange student

I'm afraid my wife will find out

I just can't keep up with all those new stamps

I'm ready to make a move on your room-mate

I'm joining the Aryan Resistance

This just isn't fitting into my workout schedule

Your hair just doesn't match my car

✦ RATE HIS RATIONALE ✦

And HOW

OH, WELL

FROM HELL

OH, WELL	FROM HELL
over dinner	over your birthday dinner
he called you	he said "I'll call you"
he called you	he called you from her home sauna
he wrote you a letter	he posted a message on alt.singles
he wrote you a song	he dedicated a song ("Another One Bites the Dust") to you on national Top 40 radio countdown
he moved his stuff out	he moved your stuff out
he asked your previous ex for advice first	he asked your previous ex to do it for him
he tried to be respectful and courteous	he tried to be respectful and courteous because, he said, "I'll be needing a reference for my next relationship"
he left a message on your machine	he left an outgoing message on his machine

PERSONALS

WHAT TO EXPECT WHEN YOU'RE REJECTED:

Your Reaction

How you respond in the immediate has direct bearing on how you'll fare in the aftermath. Agony prolonged now is agony prolonged later. Talking him out of it is humiliating and self-defeating, talking him through it is humiliating and self-effacing, and talking at all when your heart has just been ripped from your ribcage and stuffed between your molars is, well, unintelligible.

But do your best to say your piece, whatever it is; otherwise, before you know it, you'll be saying it to Rolonda. Your goal here is to be left with a feeling of just plain yuck, rather than a towering stack of unfinished business. Here are some possible ways of responding, some likelier than others.

just plain yuck   **unfinished business**

"Dr. Joyce Brothers"	**"Dorothy Parker, delayed"**	**"Cleopatra (Queen of Denial)"**
Be so cool, insightful, and articulate about the whole thing that he, impressed, will change his mind right then and there.	Wait 7 minutes after he leaves, then think of the most brilliant and withering thing anyone ever said.	"God, he's gorgeous when he's packing his bags."

ASSEMBLY LINES

You may have held the temporary misconception that your *breakup was unique,* the *worst, a previously uncharted territory of hell on earth. You may have thought briefly that you'd reached new depths of the dumps, new heights of hurt, that the things you said and heard truly revolutionized the rhetoric of resentment.*

But at the same time, didn't you have this weird feeling of déjà-dump*?—that you'd heard this before, that you were quoting yourself (or Elizabeth Taylor)?*

Truth is, breakups are all cuts of the same cheap cloth, different flavors of the same softserv, wormy crabapples from the same tree. What follows is a handy diagram you can use for proof—or future reference...

I. Intro

(select one):

I'VE BEEN THINKING ABOUT THIS FOR A WHILE, AND

THIS IS HARD FOR ME TO SAY, BUT

I THINK YOU MIGHT AGREE THAT

DON'T TAKE THIS PERSON-ALLY, BUT

THERE'S SOMETHING I'VE BEEN MEANING TO TELL YOU SINCE OUR MEETING WITH THE CALLIGRAPHER:

MY MOTHER HAS SOME-THING TO TELL YOU:

"DO YOU ACCEPT THE CHARGES?"

II. Subject + Verb

(select one from each column)

[im]personal pronoun	+	helping/hurting verb (+ N'T)
I		CAN'T
YOU		WON'T
HE		SHOULDN'T
SHE		DOESN'T
WE		DON'T
THEY		ISN'T AREN'T
THIS		AIN'T
IT		AM/ARE/IS
Y'ALL		

III. Clause of independence

(select one from each category and subcategory):

verb/predicate		clause
GO	ON	LIKE THIS
		LIVING THIS LIE
		THAT TALK SHOW ABOUT "AMERICA'S CUTEST COUPLES"
		TOP OF YOU ANYMORE
BE		THE BOY/GIRLFRIEND YOU DESERVE
		THERE FOR YOU ANYMORE
		SEEN WITH YOU ANYMORE
		MIXED UP WITH THE LIKES OF YOU IF I EVER WANT TO PASS MUSTER WITH THE SENATE JUDICIARY COMMITTEE
IN LOVE	WITH	YOU ANYMORE
		MYSELF
		MY PERSONAL TRAINER
		THE LORD
HAVE	THE	SPACE I NEED
		SAME GOALS
		TIME FOR A RELATIONSHIP
		TIME FOR SEX *AND* COMMUNICATION
HELP	BUT YOU	FEEL THAT IT'S NOT MEANT TO BE
		FEEL THAT IT'S TIME TO MOVE ON
		WONDER WHAT THE HELL I'M DOING WITH YOU
		GET OVER HIM/HER
		MOVE YOUR STUFF OUT
		CONCEAL YOUR IDENTITY FROM "THE JACKAL" ANY LONGER
FIT	INTO	MY FUTURE PLANS
		MY FAMILY
		MY FUTON
		MY ADDRESS BOOK
FAIR TO		ME
		YOU
		EITHER OF US
		MY ANT FARM
		CHUCK WOOLERY

BREAKUP ✏ QUIZ #0

Sentence Completions

1. Even though things are pretty much over for both of us and we both know we're ready to move on, I sort of haven't quite exactly broken up with him because _____ .

   a) I can't find his phone number

   b) he owes me money

   c) Mercury is in retrograde

   d) ...that *dimple!*

   e) I promised I'd see all nine *Star Wars* movies with him

   f) other _____

   g) all of the above

   h) OTHER: This question doesn't even apply. He's history.

2. I broke up with that _____ because _____ .

   a) creep...I did, okay?

   b) great guy...he can't type

   c) great guy...I'm clearly deranged

   d) OTHER: Break up with him?! I made a *promise* about those *Star Wars* movies!

3. He broke up with me during _____ .

   a) the last scene of *Dirty Dancing*

   b) the bachelor party

   c) a game of "I Dare You to Break Up with Me"

4. This sentence is incomplete because
   _____ .

   a) I am unable to read, as tears have
      soldered my contact lenses to my
      eyeballs

   b) I can't hold this book and eat
      Lik 'm' Stix at the same time

   c) we just talked—oh, wouldn't you
      know, it was all a big mistake! And
      right now we're getting ready to go
      sailing!

If you answered a-g for Question 1, d for Question 2, c for Question 3, and c for Question 4...

PLEASE . . . WAKE US WHEN IT'S OVER.

You are either in (a) denial, or (b) a satisfactory relationship.

If you chose any other answers, you have crossed the breakup border.

WELCOME TO

Splitsville,

**POPULATION 3
(you, Ben, and Jerry).**

Please move on to Chapter 1.

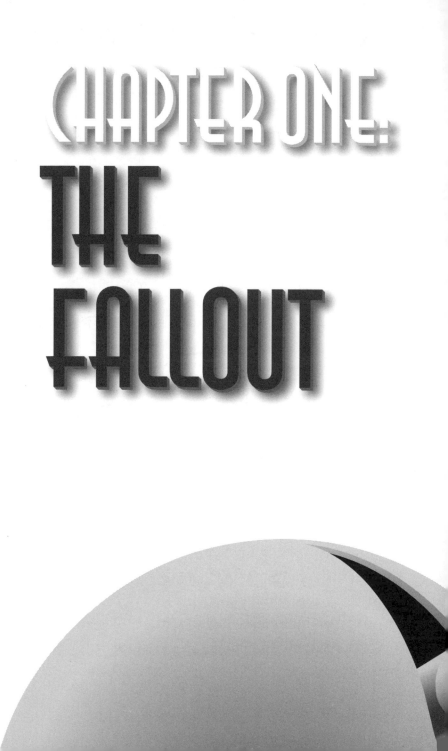

CHAPTER ONE:
THE
FALLOUT

*The world's most elite
astrophysicists recently confirmed
that black holes do exist.*

*You could have
told them that.*

SURVIVING

THE FIRST FEW DAYS...

Important Pointers

Make no crucial decisions about your life, except

(a) what your next meal will be, and

(b) that you will never love/be loved again.

Set small, attainable goals for each day; record your accomplishments in a journal.

Wednesday — I got up.

Do not bother listening over and over to the tapes he made for you (or playing them back-wards). You won't find any "clues."

always & foreve

Reprogram your telephone's automatic dial. Replace his phone number with one of the following:

(a) restaurant with free delivery

(b) the one man in your life who always answers on the first ring and seems to know exactly what to say*, or

(c) 1-900-BEEF-CAK

---

* the weather guy

HIGHLIGHTS OF YOUR SCHEDULE

Day one.

Day two.

Morning (in Alaska, anyway): Woke up.
Had weird dream about dolphins in a
library. If that was a dream, maybe the
breakup was too. No, they both probably
happened. Note for novel: those perform-
ing dolphins and I have a lot in common—great heaving and lurching, punc-
tuated with painful slaps and periods of
suffocation. Doing humiliating tricks and

HIGHLIGHTS OF YOUR SCHEDULE

chirping merrily for a guy in a funny suit. Subsisting on a diet of nothing but ... okay, I'm getting carried away.

Afternoon: Tried to watch television. Not much on besides golf. No can do; color green reminded me of him. Flipped through channels, convinced that everyone on TV knows what happened. Fairly certain that lady saying her shampoo is "gentle enough to be used every day" is actually talking about me. Kicked myself again for getting involved, turned off television. Called: several girlfriends, special friend-boy, and Mom. Told them I wasn't up to talking about it right now. Talked about it, on both lines, until telephone practically too hot to hold without oven mitt.

Evening: Girls' Night In! Breakup brigade arrived with Thelma and Louise; the Cosmo quiz; Victoria's Secret catalogs; s'mores ingredients; Playgirl; home perm, henna, and highlighting kits; Our Bodies Our Selves; the complete Judy Blume oeuvre; James Taylor and k.d. lang boxed sets; a Pulsin' Pleasure Pal; 4 DD batteries; case of kiwi-strawberry wine coolers.

Told them thanks a million, but I'd rather just drink warm beer and shoot tin cans off the porch railing with my BB gun.

INDEX
A B
C D
E F
G H
I J
K L
M N
O P
Q
R S
T U V
W X Y Z

Day three.

Morning and afternoon: Back at work! Thank goodness for Casual Day! Received compliments ("You have such a sense of style. I could never pull that off.") on plaid flannel "sarong" (my bathrobe).

Evening: Began ambitious cooking project involving basmati rice and cheesecloth. Realized I don't have any basmati rice. Cried. Convinced myself that not only do I not have any basmati rice now, I will never have any basmati rice, and no basmati rice will ever want me to have it. Furthermore, my parents' friends will start to ask them if I have any basmati rice, like my younger sister already does. Parents will muster some cheer and respond, "Nope, not yet. But she's working on it!" Mom will call and say, "You are working on it, aren't you?"

Late evening: Used cheesecloth to cover my hair and ran out for a sandwich.

Day four and beyond.

see LOOKING AHEAD, below.

INDEX

AB

CD

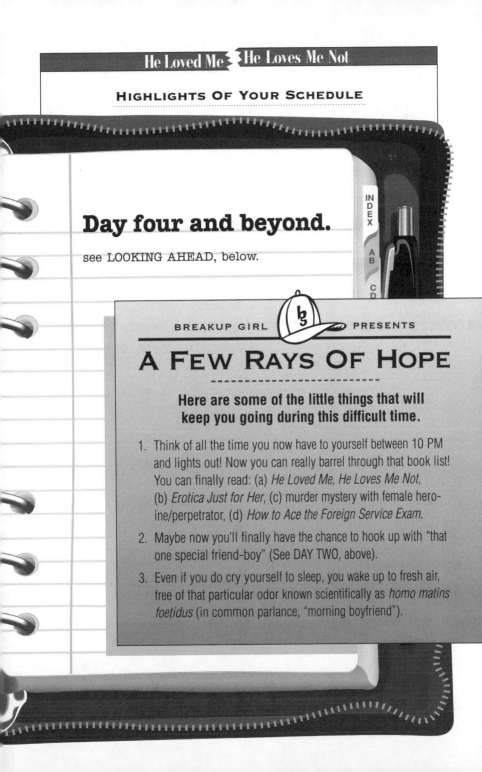

BREAKUP GIRL PRESENTS

A FEW RAYS OF HOPE

Here are some of the little things that will keep you going during this difficult time.

1. Think of all the time you now have to yourself between 10 PM and lights out! Now you can really barrel through that book list! You can finally read: (a) *He Loved Me, He Loves Me Not*, (b) *Erotica Just for Her*, (c) murder mystery with female heroine/perpetrator, (d) *How to Ace the Foreign Service Exam.*

2. Maybe now you'll finally have the chance to hook up with "that one special friend-boy" (See DAY TWO, above).

3. Even if you do cry yourself to sleep, you wake up to fresh air, free of that particular odor known scientifically as *homo matins foetidus* (in common parlance, "morning boyfriend").

Looking Ahead

Within several days, one or more of the following urges will strike.

1. Housekeeping

Immediate Steps: These hints will help you satisfy the urge—without spending money on actual redecorating.

a) Take comfy high-waisted cotton briefs and grubby flannel nightwear out of cold storage. Wear all day to prevent shopping/spying excursions.

b) Begin right away to make use of newly available storage space on vacated side of bed/futon.

c) Give away all plants that bear phallic protuberances.

d) Polish all your shoes, using his toothbrush.

e) Select one finite, manageable area for a major cleaning, such as the car where you did it, the shower where you did it, or the kitchen floor where you did it. (Save any hair samples retrieved for voodoo doll project, p.118).

2. Getting a pet

Warning: Do not go shopping when you are in a bad mood, or you will come home with a hermit crab.

3. Signing up for adult education classes

Recommendation: Stick with something neutral, like "The Cooking of the Andes." Registering for "Old Maids Have It Made: A Workshop for Single Seniors" would be precipitous.

4. Calling him to tell him you're not talking to him.

Alternative: Send him a note explaining why you think the two of you shouldn't talk at all for a little while. At the end of the note, ask him to call you to confirm that he received it.

5. Getting back together.

Note: This impulse will fade when you notice how thoroughly you are enjoying 1(b) above.

How He May React

Contrary, perhaps, to popular belief, ex-boyfriends are human. They hath eyes, hands, dimensions, passions. They are fed with the same food, hurt with the same weapons, subject to the same diseases. If you prick them, they bleed. If you dump them, they go on talk shows.

No matter which one of you did the deed, you can at least be sure that his subsequent behavior—as part of a character-redefining campaign to assert his [in]depend-ence—will be either (a) "him" to the max (e.g., trying heli-skiing), or (b) "so *not* him" (e.g., trying on your dress-es). In any case, his responses may fit into one or more of the following categories (A-E or F):

A. Filling the Time

- he'll finally start that mantelpiece beer can pyramid he's been dreaming of building
- he will start to *really love* his job
- he'll become an on-line cyberweenie

B. Bugging You

- he will goatee or de-goatee, depending on which one you hate
- he will create a World Wide Web page fea-turing a picture of you wearing "tinted" acne medication
- he will try to sell your stuff in the campus center
- he will call the woman you hate most (Bonus: even if noth-ing's "going on," he will let her wear the one thing of his that he wouldn't let you wear)
- he will call the woman you love most (mother: no; sister or best friend: not out of the realm of possibility)

C. Self-Discovery

- he will reassert guyness by: purchasing season tickets, skeet shooting, betting on horses, smashing thumb with hammer, joining rotisserie baseball league, attempting to fix transmission
- he will get a dog, vowing he's through with dating
- he will begin to write bitter, cryptic verse and join the "poetry slam" circuit
- he will take up a creative, sensitive new hobby (or career goal) that is genuinely fascinating and inspiring to him and to anyone he discusses it with

D. Trying to Get You Back

- he will take up a creative, sensitive new hobby (or career goal) that is genuinely fascinating and inspiring to him and to anyone he discusses it with
- he will get you a matching dog, thinking that it will remind you of him (and make you "need" him for tick removal)
- he will goatee or de-goatee, depending on which one you love
- he will tell you for the first time that he really likes you

E. Trying to Get Someone Else

- he will be spotted with a trophy date (dead giveaway: he will escort her someplace unlikely for a date, but likely for a sighting by one of your spies, e.g., Lady Fitness, *Little Women*, Manicurama)
- he will be spotted in the bookstore conspicuously reading *What to Do with Your First Million*
- he will start walking his dog near "Hooters"

---------- **OR** --------------

F. Hello?!

He will think you're kidding and, after giving you a few hours of "space," will call you that night.

WHAT HIS FRIENDS WILL DO

1. Take him out, get him drunk, take him home (or bail him out)
2. Call you to let you know what bad shape he's in
3. Call you back to find out if you still need someone to take his Pink Floyd ticket

The Stuff Summit

Returning all stuff to its rightful owner increases the possibility of establishing healthy closure, cleaning the slate, and of making one ex cry upon noticing the vacant space in the bathroom left by the other ex's contact lens solution. Getting and giving back everything—well, almost everything—is generally advised, unless one of you has already (a) moved without leaving a forwarding address, (b) returned home to an eviction notice or "CONDEMNED" sign, or (c) worked the items in question into a critically acclaimed performance art piece. ⬇

Getting Your Stuff Back

The toothbrush you can replace, the diaphragm may lie fallow for a spell anyway, but it's the *principle* of the thing. You may choose among three methods of stuff retrieval:

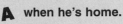

Go to his house

A when he's home.

> **CON:** He's home.
>
> **PRO:** *Carpe hombre!* (See "The Relapse," p. 138)

B when he's not home.

> **CON:** No opportunity for "relapse."
>
> **PRO:** Opportunity to skim leftovers and duplicate items from refrigerator.

Have him come by your house.

> **CON:** Must cram calendar, spiff up home, purchase/borrow cologne, and organize call-ins in time for his 7:30 PM arrival.
>
> **PRO:** He'll see from the crammed calendar left open on your desk, assorted home-spiffing projects, "Escape for Men" applied liberally to your sofa, and constantly ringing phone that you're doing just fine without him.

Meet and carry out the exchange at a neutral place, such as a convenience store parking lot, or Switzerland. This method is recommended if he can't remember where you live, or if there's never anything good in his fridge.

> **CON:** Can't necessarily trust one another to bring everything.
>
> **PRO:** Slurpees/good skiing.

Next Time, Plan Ahead

We hope, of course, that there won't *be* a next time. But just for the record, let's just say that the next time you intend to bail out of a relationship, a little planning will help you get a graceful, efficient head start on the whole stuff rigmarole. Some pointers:

• Prior to dropping the bomb, develop and memorize a direct exit path from his home based on what you've learned from Dick Van Dyke fire-safety commercials. The route should include brief stops at the locations of your belongings, which should be limited in number and value and easily accessible (see below).

• If you must keep something of value at his place, leave it out where it can be easily seized with one hand, without opening or reaching into anything, such as a box or drawer. This way, you can slide your earrings smoothly off the dresser rather than add clumsy seconds of rummaging to your otherwise poised departure.

Exception: If you have been assigned a drawer, keep *all* of your things in it. This plan offers the elegantly simple option of merely removing the drawer itself from the bureau as you leave.

What To Do With His Stuff

Having his stuff at your disposal presents several opportunities for you to support and enrich your community.

Recycling! Don't just toss his non-combustible items in the garbage! Minimize waste by returning them to him so that he can reuse the same materials to clutter someone else's house.

Donations to the less fortunate! Offer his clothes to the local ladies' quilting bee.

Multicultural events! Use his acoustic guitar as a piñata.

Visual arts! Using "found objects" for your materials, explore—and push the limits of—the media of papier mâché, tie-dye, batik, soldering, and hot wax.

Religious activities! Allow yourself one item for a shrine to his memory. Examples: photo keychain, pressed corsage, original slip of paper he gave you his number on, Sega system.

ALLOCATION OF OTHER PROPERTIES:

There Goes The Neighborhood

So that's why they're called "haunts." When the relationship is six feet under, the undead come out to prowl your favorite old hot spots. You can't walk past the park without sighting The Ghost of Picnics Past; you can't enter the brew pub without feeling the clammy presence of The Ghost of Dumb Arguments that Signaled Problems Yet to Come.

So there are some places where you don't want to go. And then there are the places you just *can't* go because, somehow, you know they're "his." This understanding is what will compel you to go seven miles out of the way to shop at the other hardware store, or to avoid the west side of town altogether.

But you have territorial rights, too. You're entitled to make a dignified bid for your fair share of properties, actual and intellectual. Be aware that this transaction may require careful thought and delicate diplomacy. Granting him the dry cleaner near his office is a simple concession, but some negotiations can get a lot more subtle and complex: Who gets the gym? Who gets the weekly "Simpsons"-watching at your mutual friends' house? Who gets skiing? Cape Cod? Graceland? The book idea?

Here's a way to settle the score. Meet in a neutral

place (ideally, neither of you will yet have laid claim to Switzerland), and bring along the wheel below. Flip a coin to see who goes first, and start spinning! Take turns until all the property is allocated. It's the only way to divide things up fair and square, even steven. Using the spinner will allow you to keep your mediations civil and avoid involving lawyers or your local chamber of commerce. It should help prevent future confusion, confrontation, and indecorous escalations on either side, such as asking friends to create "settlements" by moving into still-disputed territories, or leading walking tours of sexually historic neighborhoods.

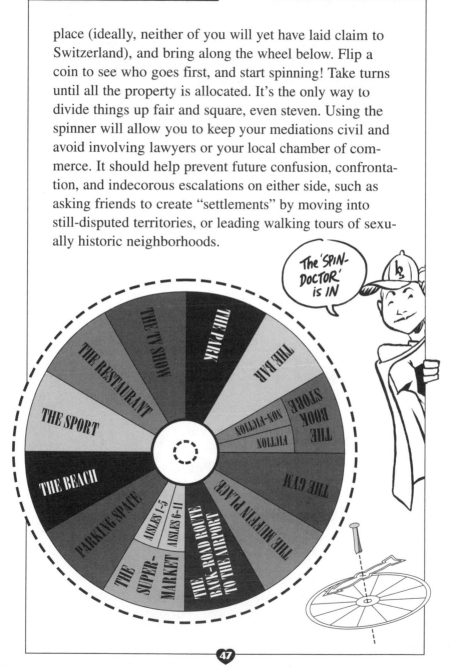

PET⚾PEEVES

Breakup Girl's parents (who believe they might have a chance of being grandparents sometime this century if their daughter would only go by some name other than "Breakup Girl") hold fast to the notion that raising a puppy is an essential dress rehearsal for raising a child. Even for dating couples with uncertain futures, a pet—his, hers, or theirs—can take on the role of child or stepchild. And in doomed relationships, those pets, much like kids, can find themselves caught in the middle (though occasionally some unhappy couples stick it out, offering resolute explanations such as, "We're staying together for the chickens"). Here, a pet owner's/disowner's guide to how our beasts may bear our burdens.

1. Your Pet

Most cats will be oblivious to any change, unless you, distracted, are late with dinner. (You may wish to contrive this delay on purpose so that your pet's insistence on being fed will at least indicate that *someone* needs you.) But any cat who, doglike, does detect your sadness, may try to elevate your spirits by presenting you with a custom-decapitated woodland creature. In keeping with her commitment to decorum, Breakup Girl advises against "recycling" this small sacrifice into a prop for a graphic revenge plot of your own.

DOG

Dogs (particularly collies) have an uncanny way of knowing when "someone's hurt." Your dog, *UNLIKE CERTAIN PEOPLE*, will thus remain ever more faithful, adoring, and true during this time. Unfortunately, your dog will have no idea that she is no longer to feel similarly toward *CERTAIN PEOPLE*. When you meet your ex by chance or for a stuff-rendezvous, your pooch's jubilant slobbering greeting will no doubt lessen the impact of your glacial stare. To deprogram, you could begin storing together—and thus mingling the scents of—items such as your ex's socks and your dog's veterinary supplies. Your dog may thus learn to associate your ex not with a good game of Frisbee, but with a dreaded heartworm pill. You might also find a way to train your pet to act as, say, a Seeing-Steve dog, who will alert you to the approach of your ex's scent, footstep, or vehicle.

OTHER PETS

If you have a horse, call in sick. Then ride bareback over the fog-swirled moors, thunderous hoofbeats rivaling the rumblings of a gathering storm, your fire-red locks whipping behind you like a defiant conqueror's flag...rebound not into the bronzed arms of the mysterious raven-haired stablehand, *no*—ride away alone to the edge of tomorrow, savoring your liberation from the chains of love that bound you and your destiny. You'll feel a lot better.

BREAKUP GIRL'S PET PEEVES

2. His Pet

Whether your ex has the commonest retriever or the rarest miniature Great Dane, you will start to see clones of his dog everywhere you look. Furthermore, you may experience a somewhat Pavlovian reaction: that is, when you see a dog that resembles your ex's, you will start to drool.

Not many single men have their own cats. Actually, it's kind of cute when they do. Oh, well.

If your ex didn't have a pet before, he may now attempt to assert his identity as a macho-single-guy/sensitive-90s-dad by buying and nurturing a Burmese python or Siamese fighting fish. You will (a) think he is really weird, and (b) think you are really weird for actually having jealous twinges of feeling "replaced."

BREAKUP GIRL'S PET PEEVES

3. "Our" Pet

Now this is where things get real complicated. If, for example, the name you chose for your little miracle is the Navajo word for "the stray cat we took in together on the first anniversary of a love that will last forever," you will have to think fast. And, of course, there's the question of who gets to keep it. Be sure to consider all the pros and cons. If your ex gets custody, you are spared all sorts of painful associations and ethical quandaries (if you walk it with someone else, is that cheating?). If you get custody, that means you offer a more stable home and are a better person. How to decide? Some couples use an age-old technique based upon the wisdom of Solomon, the drama of Brecht, and the Drew Barrymore movie *Poison Ivy*: placing the creature between the two of you and letting it choose for itself. Before using this method, you may wish to practice saying "Come!" while imitating the sound of a can opener. But if the pet does turn its tail on you, it's no big thing. Remember: dogs and cats, given a choice, also run full-speed toward moles and squashed opossums.

GETTING EVEN
→ WITHOUT ←
Getting In Trouble

Nobody likes a sore loser. No matter how low he's acted or how low you feel, stoop to nothing: avoid any unseemly behavior. You must take the high road at all times. After all, if he's been that much of a evil troll, having gone out with him at all is not exactly glowing PR for you to begin with. You've got a reputation to protect—if not resurrect. Strive for elegance, wit, and splendid little moments of chutzpah when necessary. Here are some suggestions, in order of audacity, for sweet, discreet revenge. Step right up and test your nerve!

test your
NERVE

THE
CHUTZPA-
METER

CHUTZPAH!

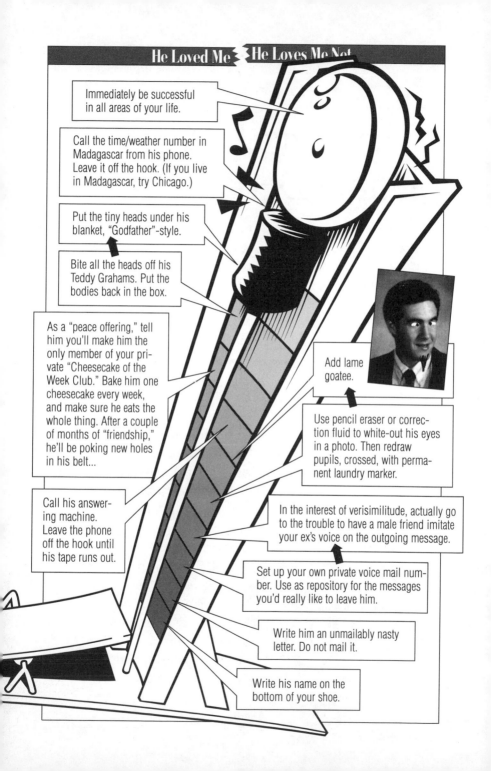

TOO FAR FOR COMFORT:

The Long-Distance Dump Debate

We're constantly encouraged to expand our horizons. Go to sleep-away camp! Attend college in another state! Hitchhike through Europe after graduation! Accept an unpaid internship in another state so that you can live away from home for the summer and still have your parents pay the rent!

Inevitably, we come away from these experiences with progressive souls, precious photo albums, padded resumes—and passionate long-distance relationships. We do have more and more tools for maintaining them (faxes, phone volume discounts, electronic mail, video teleconferencing), and we do hear long-distance success stories (the summer fling that lasted a lifetime, the professors with bi-coastal tenure, *WOMAN WEDS ALIEN*).

But in general, the long-distance mortality rate is much higher, it seems, than that of close-range romance. Long-distance relationships tend to languish under the issue of who visits whom, the question of "seeing other people," and the pressure of making every minute totally amazing when you finally are together. It's no surprise when long-distancers make the decision to turn off the life support and put the veg-

WEAKLY WILD NEWS Theory of Relativity dooms starcrossed lovers...

LYNN & ALIEN SPLITSVILLE!

She: "Hellish Commute!"

It: "Need My Space!"

Happy Couple shocks NASA

etable out of its misery.

Just how harsh is the long-distance dump? At first glance, it does seem like a snap compared to the regional rejection: there's less of him to miss, none of him to run into unprepared, and so on. But if you're in the thick of it, you know better—and you can be the first to tell your lone-lier-than-thou pals that it's no rest-stop picnic. Below, some talking points for the debate over who's more bumming.

WHY LONG-DISTANCE BREAKUPS ARE

BETTER THAN CLOSE-RANGE	WORSE THAN CLOSE-RANGE
significant increase in time available to explore and enjoy your own neighborhood	significant decrease in frequent flier miles
significant decrease in phone bill	phone bill scored you frequent flier miles
you can finally sell your car	gas card scored you frequent flier miles
scary chance meetings much less likely	"chance" meetings much scarier; means he "just happened" to hitchhike across two time zones
since he's not normally around, you don't notice that he's missing as much	short of a long-range military radar system, no efficient way of tracking his whereabouts
new justification for buying clothes that "don't travel well"	now no justification for buying cute "travel size" cosmetics
loads of free time on weekends	loads of free time on weekends

The Breakup Princess Phone

■ Letter-free buttons prevent you from deciding that what phone numbers spell "means something"

■ Built-in chip stores his answering machine message so you won't be charged for every local call you make "just to hear his voice"

■ "Yes, it's working" indicator light

■ Small size, easily carried from room to room or stowed in garbage disposal

■ Redial button: not only calls back the number you just dialed, but also allows you to take back what you just said

■ Mirror: helps you look your best—and saves you a trip—when he calls

Built-in Services:

- **ThinkTwice**™ blocks you from calling him when you're sniffling, hungry, or "in the mood"

- **Busybody signal**: custom ring alerts you to caller who can't be trusted not to misinterpret/spread the word about your state of mind

- **Twenty-three-way-calling**: allows you to explain "what happened" to all mid-level acquaintances at once

- **Call waiting, and waiting, and waiting...**: Comes with assortment of magazines and herbal teas

- **Caller id**: Custom ring identifies caller who, acting on the pleasure principle and the drive for instant gratification, is phoning to "get you out to do something fun." Also available: **caller ego** (custom ring identifies cute boy who is really nice to you); **caller superego** (your mother)

- **Call answering**: allows for custom outgoing messages, such as: "If this is Robin or Stacey, push 1. If you're calling to tell me I did the right thing, push 2. If this is Carl, don't push it."

PITY POSTCARDS

Your telephone: companion or curse?

During peak boyfriend, the telephone is a throbbing, pulsing, love machine. During peak breakup, it is a lifeline...except when you decide you'd rather die than talk about this whole thing again right now. Your throat hurts, your jaw aches, you are beginning to slur your speech. It's time to turn off that ringer for a spell. But what to do, you ask, about certain urgent communications that must get through?...Well, you may have nodes on your larynx, but you still have needs. Use these postcards to make sure they're met.

PITY POSTCARDS

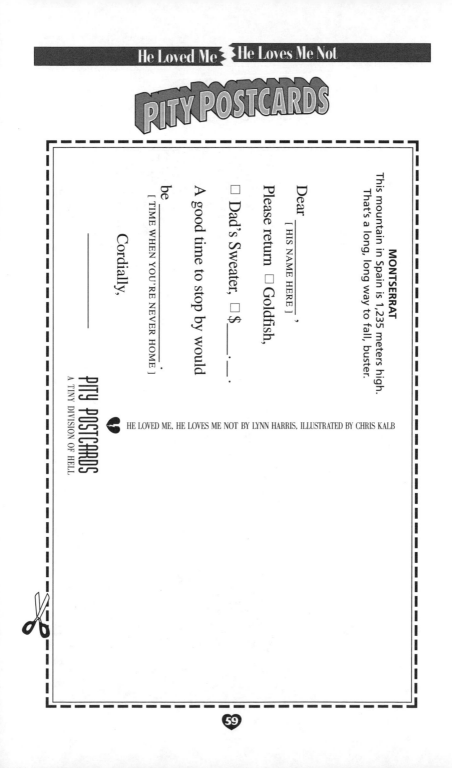

MONTSERRAT
This mountain in Spain is 1,235 meters high.
That's a long, long way to fall, buster.

Dear _____,
[HIS NAME HERE]

Please return ☐ Goldfish,

☐ Dad's Sweater, ☐ $ ____ . ___ .

A good time to stop by would

be _____.
[TIME WHEN YOU'RE NEVER HOME]

Cordially,

_____

PITY POSTCARDS
A TINY DIVISION OF HELL.

HE LOVED ME, HE LOVES ME NOT BY LYNN HARRIS, ILLUSTRATED BY CHRIS KALB

PITY POSTCARDS

PITY POSTCARDS

PITY POSTCARDS

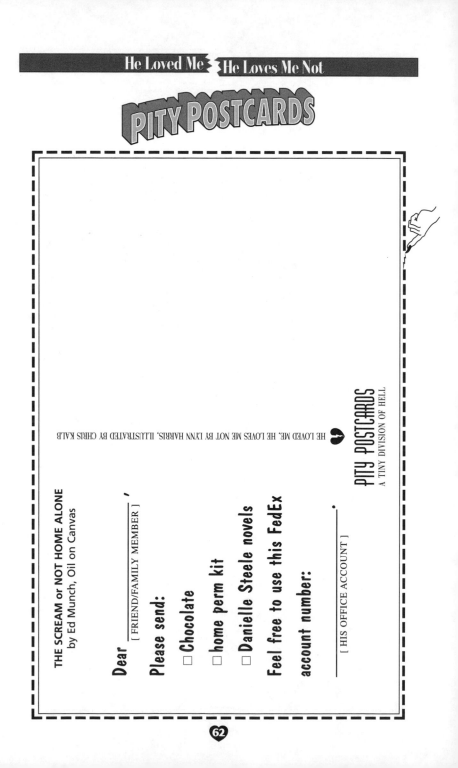

THE SCREAM or NOT HOME ALONE
by Ed Munch, Oil on Canvas

Dear _____ ,
[FRIEND/FAMILY MEMBER]

Please send:

☐ Chocolate

☐ home perm kit

☐ Danielle Steele novels

Feel free to use this FedEx

account number:

_____ .
[HIS OFFICE ACCOUNT]

HE LOVED ME, HE LOVES ME NOT, BY LYNN HARRIS, ILLUSTRATED BY CHRIS KALB

PITY POSTCARDS
A TINY DIVISION OF HELL

PITY POSTCARDS

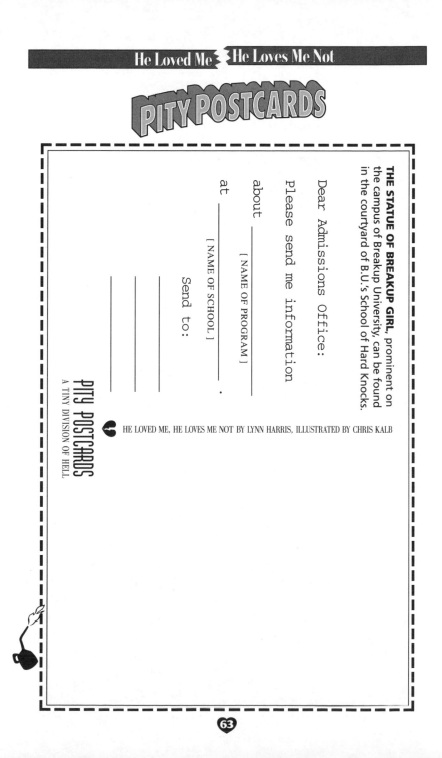

THE STATUE OF BREAKUP GIRL, prominent on the campus of Breakup University, can be found in the courtyard of B.U.'s School of Hard Knocks.

Dear Admissions Office:

Please send me information

about _____

[NAME OF PROGRAM]

at _____

[NAME OF SCHOOL]

.

Send to:

_____

_____

_____

PITY POSTCARDS
A TINY DIVISION OF HELL.

HE LOVED ME, HE LOVES ME NOT BY LYNN HARRIS, ILLUSTRATED BY CHRIS KALB

PITY POSTCARDS

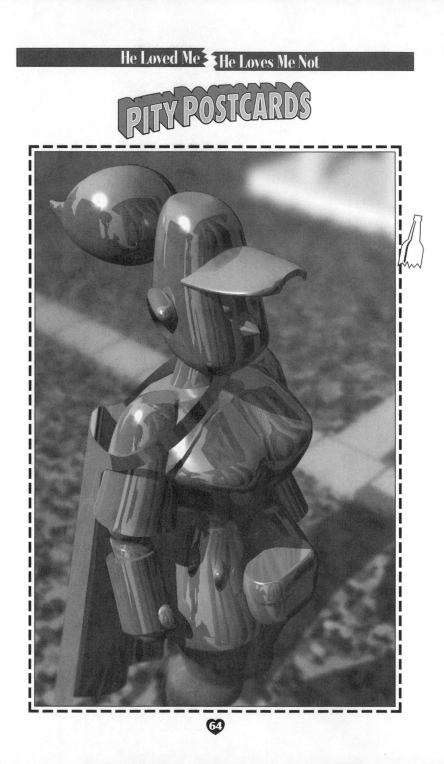

PITY POSTCARDS

PITY POSTCARDS

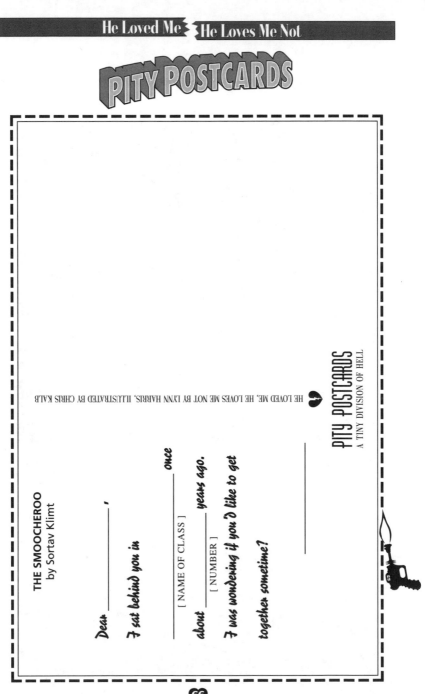

THE SMOOCHEROO
by Sortav Klimt

Dear _____,

I sat behind you in _____ once

[NAME OF CLASS]

about _____ years ago.

[NUMBER]

I was wondering if you'd like to get

together sometime?

PITY POSTCARDS
A TINY DIVISION OF HELL

HE LOVED ME, HE LOVES ME NOT BY LYNN HARRIS, ILLUSTRATED BY CHRIS KALB

Free Association

Objective

Challenge a friend to name one word that *doesn't* remind you of him.

Directions

1. Your "opponent" selects and suggests a randomly chosen word without any obvious association to you, romance, or your relationship.

   Example: "sunset"

2. Tell your "opponent" to try again.

3. Your "opponent" selects and suggests a randomly chosen word without any obvious association to you, romance, or your relationship.

   Example: "burlap"

4. You have 30 seconds to explain why that word reminds you of him.

   Rule: Responses must have actual narrative content.

   Acceptable response: "The potato sacks in the sack races at the company picnic where we met were made of **burlap**."

   Unacceptable response: "Rhymes with 'his-lap,' my

favorite place to sit."

5. Go back to step 3. Repeat cycle until your opponent states the following: "Okay, okay, I get the point."

6. Say, "Point...point, oh, oh, I got it, his favorite **point** guard of all time was Nate 'Tiny' Archibald of the Boston Celtics..."

~~Scoring~~ *uh, sorry*
Counting Points

Oh, let's say it's 5 points per acceptable response, 10 for any of the challenge words below. But you're going to win, anyway.

Challenge Round

If you're feeling saucy, try to dig up some bittersweet memories associated with:

pinochle - turnip - gnome - draconian - synechdoche

Other Rules

1. Do not play Free Association for money. That's not fair.

2. Do not play Free Association with him.

3. Do not play your own "Solitaire" version of Free Association.

BREAKUP 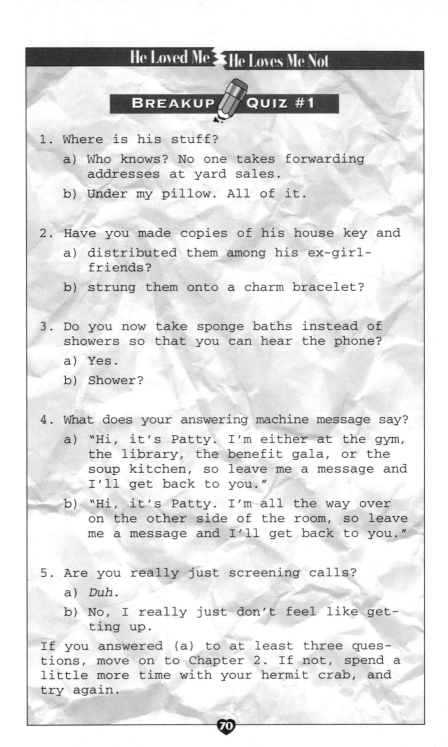 QUIZ #1

1. Where is his stuff?

   a) Who knows? No one takes forwarding addresses at yard sales.

   b) Under my pillow. All of it.

2. Have you made copies of his house key and

   a) distributed them among his ex-girl-friends?

   b) strung them onto a charm bracelet?

3. Do you now take sponge baths instead of showers so that you can hear the phone?

   a) Yes.

   b) Shower?

4. What does your answering machine message say?

   a) "Hi, it's Patty. I'm either at the gym, the library, the benefit gala, or the soup kitchen, so leave me a message and I'll get back to you."

   b) "Hi, it's Patty. I'm all the way over on the other side of the room, so leave me a message and I'll get back to you."

5. Are you really just screening calls?

   a) *Duh.*

   b) No, I really just don't feel like getting up.

If you answered (a) to at least three questions, move on to Chapter 2. If not, spend a little more time with your hermit crab, and try again.

THE CHANCE

MEETING

NUMBER ONE

WHERE:
convenience store

APPROPRIATE BODY LANGUAGE:
point at something way behind him

APPROPRIATE THING TO SAY:
"Look!"
(buys you a couple of seconds
for your getaway)

CHAPTER TWO:
"I NEVER REALIZED HOW MUCH I ENJOY SPENDING TIME ALONE"
(BREAKUP MYTH #5)

*Now you'll finally have the chance
to tackle all those household tasks, crafts,
and personal fulfillment projects
you've been meaning to get around to–
such as hauling that stack of used love letters
to white-paper recycling,
sewing your own voodoo doll,
and working your way alphabetically
through the video store.*

Home Improvement and Personal Fulfillment Projects

You now realize that for the duration of your partnership, it *never once* occurred to you to spend some quality time making your own custom line of soap-on-a-rope. So caught up in that giddy whirlwind were you, that *not once* did you think to organize those little extra-button bags by designer and diameter. How could you have let yourself get so *stifled?* How could you have let things *slide* so? Now, finally, is your chance to catch up on what's important to you, to spend some time with Numero Uno, to explore and express what's really inside.

Get into Shape!

Begin alternating daily regime of running and powerwalking. On odd days, go by his house.

Get Organized!

Cross-sort your coupons by product type and expiration date. Consider going shopping, but instead stay home and re-sort coupons by his favorite and least-favorite foods.

"If I had a hammer...oh, don't tempt me!" Carpentry Projects!

Experience the satisfaction of building something yourself from scratch or from a kit: mug rack or spice rack, birdfeeder, Roman catapult. Cautionary note: avoid pre-fab furniture kits if his name was "Alan"; use of enclosed wrenches may trigger painful associations.

Make Your Own!

Candles

Use for: seances, melodramatic late-night penning of memoirs, removing his odor from your apartment

Macrame notions

Use for: plant hangers, fashion belts, noose for his Teddy

Decorative pillows

Use for: making it look like there's someone else under the covers

Rainy Day Fun!

• Make paper-bag or sock puppets and put on a show! (Stick to fairy tales or childhood stories; audience might read too much into "Punch and Judy," passion plays, or an adaptation of "Heartburn.")

• Make "jewelry" by stringing pieces of uncooked ziti and wads of tinfoil on a pretty-colored string. Play a funny joke on your friends by wearing it the next time you go out—they'll think you've *really* "lost it!" Ha, ha!

• Make bookcovers out of paper bags. Decorate with markers, magazine cutouts, and stickers. Use as functional—and funky—way to protect/disguise valuable books such as *The Pop-Up Kama Sutra*, his complete Vonnegut collection, and your bound manuscript-in-progress (tentatively titled *Gary Hortense Mitchell of Floyd Street in Austin: One Loser's Story -or- Oops! I Swore I'd Never Tell Anyone Your Middle Name, Didn't I?*).

Who's Who
in Chocolate

BREAKUP BAR FROM THE MAKERS OF SINGLES BAR — DROWN YER SORROWS IN CHOCOLATE

Chocolate is pretty much the last thing you'd want to eat when going through a breakup.

Well, sure. Chocolate contains theobromine, an alkaloid similar to caffeine, meaning that it shares caffeine's side effects: alertness, elevated mood, depression of appetite, and increased mental and physical energy.

At this time, none of those side effects is at all desirable.

However, the second-to-last thing you want to do right now is deprive yourself of anything, even a known diuretic. So if you must have chocolate, have chocolate. Just make sure of two things: (1) before you start, read through the following so that you make the chocolate choices that are best for you, and (2) hope he doesn't get his hands on any.

- **Dark chocolate:** the red wine of chocolate; says "Damn it, I deserve a treat."

- **Milk chocolate:** the white zinfandel of chocolate; says "Damn it, I don't deserve dark chocolate."

- **Brownies:** the beer of chocolate (eat six).

- **Baking** (or "unsweetened") **chocolate** is produced early in the chocolate-making process by grinding and molding the roasted cacao seeds before sweetening or otherwise adding flavor. Used, of course, for baking, and also for eating straight out of the box on the days when you are sure you're a "bad person."

- **Cocoa butter** is the fatty, waxy substance derived from the filtration of crushed cacao seeds. If you do crave chocolate, keep some—even a handful of chips—around the house at all times; otherwise, you may be tempted to eat soap.

- **Fudge.** Don't bother making it yourself: you need obscure apparati such as a *candy thermometer*, of all things; plus you'll have to decide whether or not to wait for it to harden.

- **Chocolate milk.** Likewise, must be storebought; otherwise you'll use skim—pointless.

- **Chocolate-chip cookie dough.** Duh.

- **Chocolate-covered pretzels.** Oh, *yeah*! Sweet *and* salt—it's better than shampoo-plus-conditioner!

- **Hershey's Kisses.** Squat, malevolent morsels whose annoyance factor is surpassed only by that of candy "conversation" hearts (see page 104). Acceptable only when the "kiss" implied is the a-romantic grandmother type, as in a consolation gift from a friend.

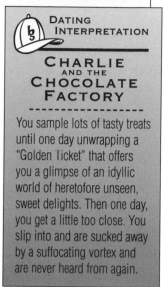

DATING INTERPRETATION

CHARLIE AND THE CHOCOLATE FACTORY

You sample lots of tasty treats until one day unwrapping a "Golden Ticket" that offers you a glimpse of an idyllic world of heretofore unseen, sweet delights. Then one day, you get a little too close. You slip into and are sucked away by a suffocating vortex and are never heard from again.

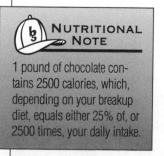

NUTRITIONAL NOTE

1 pound of chocolate contains 2500 calories, which, depending on your breakup diet, equals either 25% of, or 2500 times, your daily intake.

- **Hershey's Hugs.** Swirly, almond-blotched white/milk chocolate desecrations, a purist's lily-gilding nightmare. And the name: *Hugs* ?! Oh, please. Anyway, they are delicious.

- **M & Ms:** Relax, that thing about the green ones is a myth. (But the orange ones are good luck.)

- **Salt-'n'-Vinegar potato chips.** The antidote.

How Your Roommates *Will React*

or "Maybe Now We Can Spend More Time Together As A House"

When you're going through a breakup, don't underestimate the importance of having roommates you can count on...to burst in with a surprise swinging singles party when you've just settled down for a quiet evening with Solitaire for Windows or...to take off for so-and-so's lake house when you've just walked in with the household's bonding movie line-up and cookie dough for three, your treat.

NOW, DON'T START PACKING—THEY MEAN WELL, GOD BLESS 'EM—JUST BE PREPARED FOR ...

NOTE: He Loved Me, He Loves Me Not *makes a great gift!*

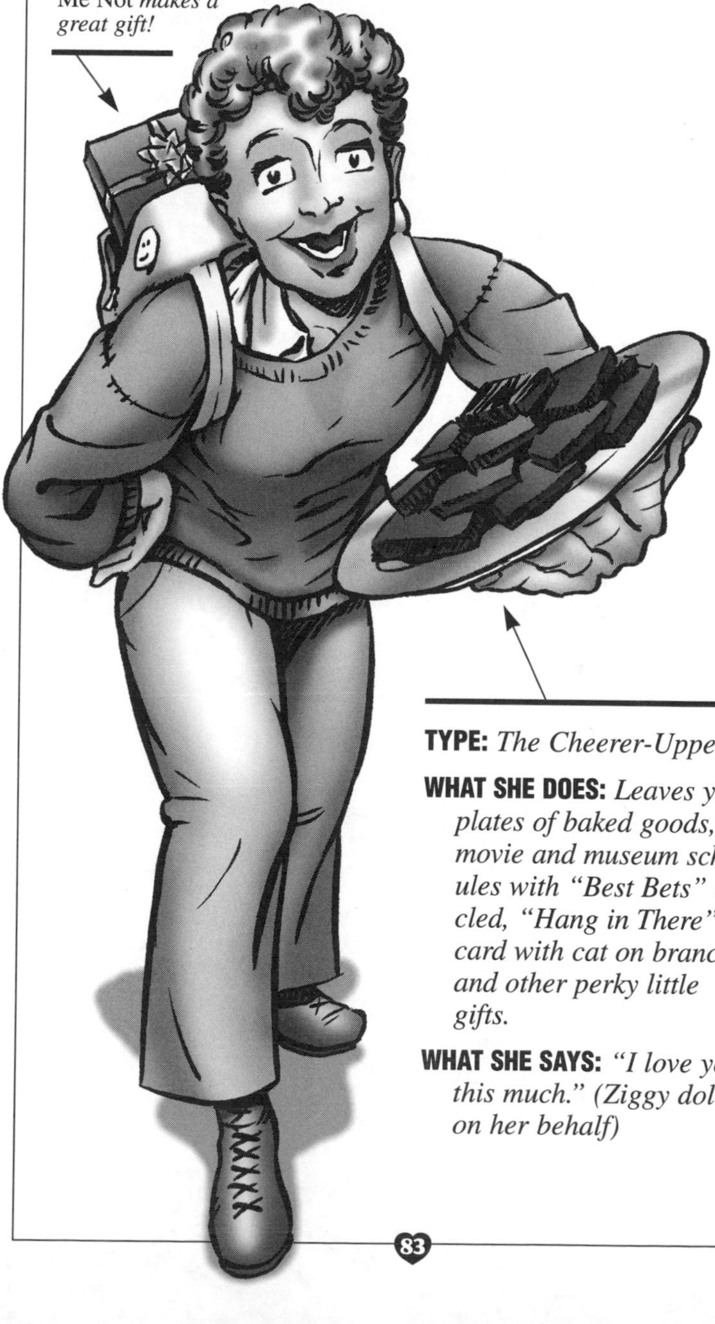

TYPE: *The Cheerer-Upper*

WHAT SHE DOES: *Leaves you plates of baked goods, movie and museum schedules with "Best Bets" circled, "Hang in There" card with cat on branch, and other perky little gifts.*

WHAT SHE SAYS: *"I love you this much." (Ziggy doll, on her behalf)*

TYPE: *The Advice-Giver*

WHAT SHE DOES: *Sits you down and gives you the same advice that she gave herself in the long talks she gave you when she went through her last breakup. Offers you her diary for reference.*

WHAT SHE SAYS: *"I totally know how you feel, because until I got over the thing with Doug, I..."*

TYPE: *The Boyfriend-Hater*

WHAT SHE DOES: *Tells you she never liked Steve anyway.*

WHAT SHE SAYS: *"Do you want to maybe hang out and do something fun sometime, like before?"*

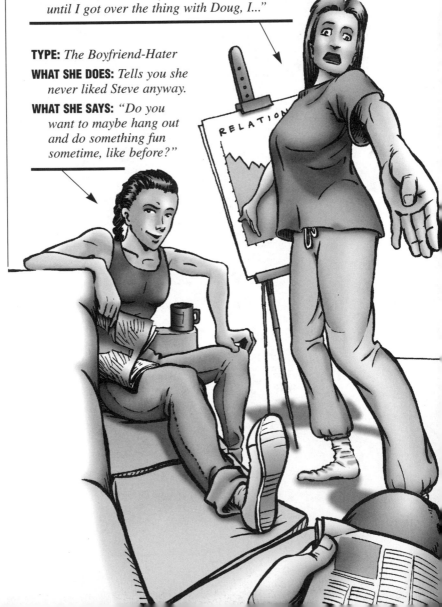

TYPE: *The Boyfriend-Haver*

WHAT SHE DOES: *Beats a hasty retreat every time you find them together anywhere in the house.*

WHAT SHE SAYS: *"Sorry, we'll be out of here in a second."*

How Your **Roommates** *Will React*

TYPE: *The Boyfriend-Lover*

WHAT SHE DOES: *Takes it as hard as you do.*

WHAT SHE SAYS: *"Would it help if I talked to him for you?"*

The Elevator Shaft:
But What If You *Work* Together?

So much for going cold turkey. Sure, you can nurture your inner spinster during your nights at home, but if you work together you just may have to see his adorable/goblin-like face every day in between.

But don't even *think* about quitting your job. Consider the perks of having him around:

1. The Status Quo.

Like any good, doomed office romance, yours was a complete secret from everyone except the swarthy, winking guy in the mailroom. That means you're already experts at avoiding one another altogether. No big change.*

2. Convenient Performance Review.

Is he suffering, celebrating, or something in between? Sharing a workplace will allow you to keep tabs, as shown in the examples at right.

3. Free Post-its™.

---

* Just for good measure, though, you may wish to follow the instructions under "Allocation of Other Properties: There Goes The Neighborhood," p. 46, in order to make certain office space arrangements official, such as: "Who gets the cafeteria? The elevator? The 'good' copier?"

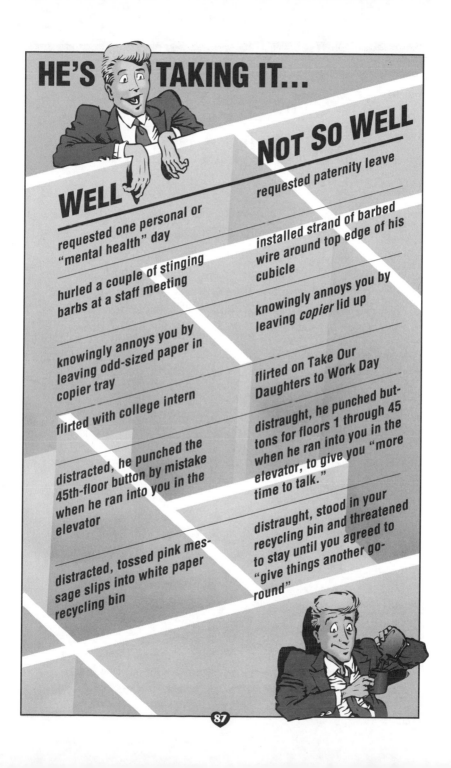

HE'S TAKING IT...

WELL

NOT SO WELL

requested one personal or "mental health" day

requested paternity leave

hurled a couple of stinging barbs at a staff meeting

installed strand of barbed wire around top edge of his cubicle

knowingly annoys you by leaving odd-sized paper in copier tray

knowingly annoys you by leaving *copier* lid up

flirted with college intern

flirted on Take Our Daughters to Work Day

distracted, he punched the 45th-floor button by mistake when he ran into you in the elevator

distraught, he punched buttons for floors 1 through 45 when he ran into you in the elevator, to give you "more time to talk."

distracted, tossed pink message slips into white paper recycling bin

distraught, stood in your recycling bin and threatened to stay until you agreed to "give things another go-round"

The AfterMath:
Breakup Algebra

Time heals.

Yeah, well that's not good enough. You need to know exactly how long this breakup business is going to last. The mathematical formula below will allow you to calculate precisely how much time will elapse before you can declare yourself "over it" (margin of error: approx. 1 boyfriend).

$$D = R \left(\frac{1}{b} + \frac{p+f}{l} + \pi s^3 \right) \times T(v + c + a)$$

D=HOW LONG IT WILL TAKE TO DISTANCE YOURSELF (in months)

R = RATE his looks on a scale from 1 to 10

T = amount of TIME you were together (months)

b = number of times you've already BROKEN UP

p = 0 if your PARENTS liked him
p = 5 if your PARENTS didn't like him

f = number of close FRIENDS you have in common, *except*
f = 1,439 if you have no other FRIENDS

l = number of miles away he LIVES, *except*
l = 0.5 if you LIVED together

s = volume of his STUFF that you're secretly keeping

v = tan (number of tropical VACATIONS you've taken together)
c = sin (number of times he CHEATED on you) {use 1/c if you cheated on him}
a = cosine (amount of money you have in joint checking ACCOUNT)

More Handy Breakup Math

1. Absolute Value

Even after the crash, your once-priceless assets are far from worthless.

For example:

	SENTIMENTAL VALUE	ABSOLUTE VALUE
HIS STEREO	lovemaking sessions lasted through all six (6) CDs	cash amount stereo with 6-CD changer brings at flea market
HIS LOVE LETTERS	reading them increased your heart rate by a factor of three (3)	cash amount handwriting analyst offers you for letters (for use in article entitled "3 Ways to Identify Losers Through Their Penmanship")

More Handy Breakup Math

2. Calculator fun!

Punch in certain numbers to create entertaining upside-down:

ⓐ insults: (if you work for him)
8075515508 = `BOSSISSLOB`

ⓑ whining: 773440 (serious) = `OhhELL`

450940 (whimsical) = `Oh60Sh`

ⓒ self-assurance, physical:
58008918 = `BIGBOOBS`

593707734 = `hELLOLE6S`

ⓓ self-assurance, mental:
550851345 = `ShEISBOSS`

3. Geometry

Prove that he occupies over 30% of the total area in your heart.

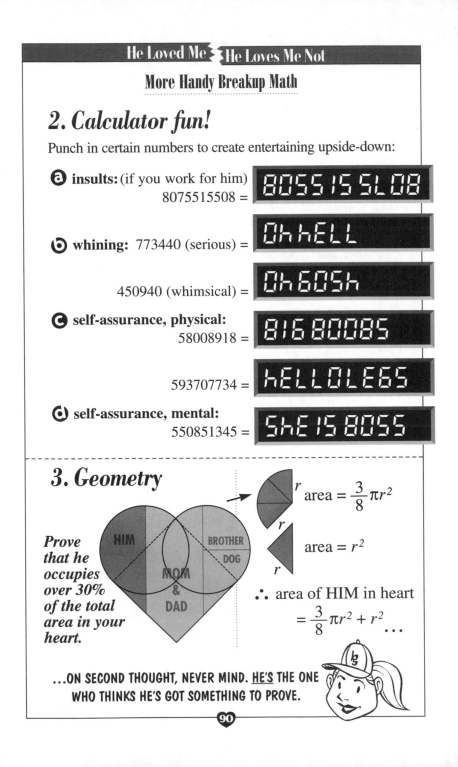

HIM   BROTHER
DOG
MOM
&
DAD

r area $= \dfrac{3}{8}\pi r^2$

r area $= r^2$

r

∴ area of HIM in heart
$= \dfrac{3}{8}\pi r^2 + r^2 \ldots$

...ON SECOND THOUGHT, NEVER MIND. HE'S THE ONE WHO THINKS HE'S GOT SOMETHING TO PROVE.

BREAKING EVEN:

Your Breakup Budget

I n these tough economic times, you can't afford to let your breakup break your bank. Not to worry. When you look at both sides of the equation, as shown below, you'll see that it is possible to balance your budget.

Important note: keep all receipts from items in "Breakup Expense" column; once you're officially the author of *I'm OK, He Sucks*, you'll need them to claim tax deductions.

BREAKING EVEN: YOUR BREAKUP BUDGET

BREAKUP EXPENSE	approx $ value	BREAKUP SAVINGS/INCOME	approx $ value	BALANCE	RUNNING TOTAL
loss of free long-distance calling privileges from his apartment/office phone	$ 75	discovery that his calling card number was someone else's measurements and zip code makes you not feel that bad about using it	$ 95	+ $ 20	$ 20
shopping expedition for something to wear when he calls	$ 140	your mother's reinstatement of your high-school clothing allowance (see p. 145), adjusted for inflation.	$350	+ $210	$230

91

BREAKUP EXPENSE	approx $ value	BREAKUP SAVINGS/INCOME	approx $ value	BALANCE	RUNNING TOTAL
new haircut, because either (a) now you can get it done the way *you* like it, or (b) you fell asleep with gummy bears on your pillow	$ 35	free cucumber eye treatment from nice lady at salon who asks if you've been crying	$15	- $ 20	$210
loss of supply of free antihistamine samples from his doctor parents	$325	he kept the cat	$215	- $110	$100
one-time purchase of comfort food	$25.68	no longer have to buy "his" 2% in addition to your skim	$27	+$1.32	$101.32
unleashing of creative instincts during time spent on your own leads to impulse purchase of Krazy Glue, blowtorch, goggles	$41	sale of your "found objects" (car keys, ski boots, vintage tuxedo) sculpture at amateur crafts festival	$50	+ $ 9	$110.32
no more free meals in nice restaurants	$200	no more offering to leave the tip for "free" meals in nice restaurants	$40	- $160	-$49.68

➡

B R E A K I N G   E V E N :   Y O U R   B R E A K U P   B U D G E T

BREAKUP EXPENSE	approx $ value	BREAKUP SAVINGS/INCOME	approx $ value	BALANCE	RUNNING TOTAL
no more free movies	$45	your roommates don't have the heart to tell you you owe for the cable bill	$45	$ 0	-$49.68
sleeping through call from temp agency	$96 (before taxes)	pawning his Sharper Image clock radio	$90	- $ 6	-$55.68
"Since you're the one who has to mess with your hormones, I'll pick up the tab for The Pill."	$79	stipend for clinical trial of The Boyfriend Patch	$135	+ $ 56	$ 0.32
				subtotal	$ 0.32
		roommates go ahead and ask if you have a stamp they can use for the cable bill			-$ 0.32
				TOTAL BREAKUP EXPENDITURE	$ 0

YIPPIE! THE ONLY PRICE I PAY IS AN EMOTIONAL ONE!

93

Cooking With Pain:

In The Kitchen *with* Breakup Girl

Breakup Recipes!

> How abut his head on a platter?

S
ooner or later, either your brain or your stomach lining is going to let you know that your steady diet of Funyons and Pixie Stix will not give you the figure, complexion, or essential vitamins you need in order to continue making regular trips between the TV and the kitchen. Follow these simple recipes for a more balanced breakup.

MEN ARE PIGS-IN-A-BLANKET

Ingredients:

2 cups baking mix

1/2 cup cold water

8 frankfurters (could substitute tofu dogs, but they're gross)

Preheat oven to 450. Blend baking mix and water in bowl. On floured surface, form dough into a ball. Knead vigorously until you feel better.

Roll dough out into flat circle and cut into 8 wedges. Place one frankfurter on each and roll up dough around it, starting with wide end.

Bake about 15 minutes, or until the end of "Baywatch." Serve with Lots-More-Tears Hot Sauce.

– – – – –

LOTS-MORE-TEARS HOT SAUCE

Mix together any combination of:

fresh jalapeño pepper, chopped, with seeds

cayenne pepper

crushed red pepper

habanero peppers stored in protective case at West Indian market, chopped

horseradish, that good magenta color

Moisten mixture with vinegar and vegetable oil. Add salt to taste. Will keep for several weeks in refrigerator (use glass jar; may eat through Tupperware).

Refrain from using sauce in Lucy Ricardo-style slapstick revenge plot—too obvious. Instead, if you're "all cried out" but still need to inspire pity at any moment, unscrew lid and take a few eye-moistening whiffs. Conversely, if you need to keep up dry-eyed appearances, use hot sauce to explain away already existing redness, swelling.

FEAR OF COMMIT-MINT BROWNIES

Go to the store to buy brownie mix. Worry that if you settle on one particular brand, you'll never be able to switch to another. Decide to buy several boxes, just in case.

Prepare according to manufacturer's directions, adding 1/2 teaspoon peppermint extract when you feel you are ready.

TWO BRAISED DUCKS WITH ONION AND BROCCOLI PUREES, CARAMEL VINEGAR SAUCE, AND CROUTONS

Overall game plan:
• get the stock going while you clean the ducks
• prepare the duck seasoning mixture

- while ducks are cooking, prepare the purees
- while onions are cooking, prepare the veloute for the puree
- then go ahead and start the vinegar sauce and croutons

For the stock, you'll need:

> **2 tablespoons goose fat**
>
> **1/2 cup onions, sliced**
>
> **1/2 cup carrots, sliced**
>
> **3 ounces boiled ham, diced**
>
> **3 tablespoons flour**
>
> **1 cup dry white wine**
>
> **bouquet garni of parsley, thyme, and 1/2 grape leaf-**
>
> *– OH, FORGET IT*

QUADRUPLE CHOCOLATE-FUDGE CHIP MOUSSE BROWNIES A LA MODE

Prepare brownies as above. Top entire pan with: 1 bag chocolate chips, 1 pint chocolate ice cream, 1 pint chocolate mousse, hot fudge to taste.

Serves one.

- - - - -

IT'S-NOT-LIKE-I'M-GOING-TO-BE-KISSING-ANYBODY GARLIC BREAD

Take one loaf of French or Italian

bread. Make 1-inch slices crosswise, without cutting all the way through. Chop 1 head of raw garlic and blend with a stick or so of softened butter.

Spread this mixture between slices. Wrap bread in foil and bake in 400 oven until heated through.

Garnish with raw onions; serve with chips (ranch, nacho cheese, or sour cream 'n' onion).

- - - - -

HEARTBREAK HUMMUS

Ingredients:

2 cloves garlic

1 can chick peas

1/2 cup tahini (sesame seed paste)

1/2 cup olive oil

fresh parsley

lemon juice to taste

Combine all ingredients in food processor. (If you don't have one, buy one. You deserve it. Also one of those bread machines.) Blend until smooth. Attempt to season to taste.

Decide that it's okay, but not quite as authentic as you'd like. Make arrangements to live with host family and work as apprentice chef in Syria for one year.

SWEET REVENGE CHEESECAKE

(see "Getting Even Without Getting In Trouble," p. 52)

Collect cheesecake recipes from friends, family, the Internet. As a "peace offering," give one to your ex every week, with notes that say things like, "So glad that we're still friends." Given all the time you now have for exercise, you'll be fit as a fiddle, while he, sooner or later, will begin to show signs of the "just-friends 15."

Suggestion: Now and then, throw in a "low-fat" cheescake (made with lite cream cheese) to keep him from suspecting anything.

REBOUND RISOTTO

Part 1:

Invite a guy over for a premature "I'd love to make you dinner sometime" rebound date.

Part 2:

In a saucepan, bring 5 cups of stock to boil. Reduce to a simmer. In a larger pan, saute one small chopped onion in butter. Stir in 1 1/2 cups Arborio rice. Add 1/2 cup dry white wine and cook 18-20 minutes, stirring/wondering what the hell you're doing constantly. Serve with grated Parmesan.

TAKE THE "N" OUT OF "ALONE"
AND ALL YOU'VE GOT IS "ALOE"

Breakup
Girl's

Household Hints

Homewrecking and housekeeping needn't be mutually exclusive. Still, maintaining your home during a breakup does require some special domestic savvy. Here are some tips:

A. Stain Removal and Prevention

Candle wax (from shrine or vigil)

Scrape off of fabric with dull knife, iron between pieces of paper towel or bag (will absorb softened wax); launder in hot water. Wish you hadn't, wondering if patterns left by the wax, like tea leaves, might have "meant something."

Tears

 (a) fogging up contact lenses: use daily cleaner with saline, then enzyme solution; spend $450 on new Gaulthier glasses

 (b) causing mildew growth on sheets, clothing: launder with Lysol; wear shower-curtain liner around the house

 (c) mixed with mascara or eyeliner: rub detergent into stain, wash in cool water; spend $450 on new Gaulthier sunglasses

Chocolate

Rub paste of borax and water into stain; let stand, then rinse in cool water. Or, if urgent, attempt to eat.

All these and other stains

Pack everything into a suitcase and visit home; or buy new clothes.

Lipstick on his collar

Remove collar with scissors.

B. First Aid

Fainting (or "swooning"). Smelling salts are the standard treatment, but since no one knows what they are, he's just going to have to figure out some other way to remedy the impact of his words.

Bruised ego. Ice affected area with cold compress or frozen daiquiri.

Getting majorly burned. Stand in cold shower until numb. Apply aloe-vera gel. Wrap affected area in flannel, loosely, to avoid chafing. Painful blisters may develop, lasting into next relationship.

C. Household Fixit Projects

Such as: changing lightbulbs, connecting stereo, rotating in-line skate wheels, cleaning bike chain, checking oil, installing air conditioner.

Before, you stroked his guyness by letting him lend a hand—but you know how to do all this stuff already.

This Joint is Dumpin'!
Heartbreak Hits

It's the Top 40 of torture, the hymns to him, the jingles of jilt! That's right, all the songs that make it worse... all in one record collection! These are the albums you'll listen to over and over—and then store on the radiator!

Here's what you'll hear:

I Will Survive!
Gonna Wash That Man Right Out of My Hair
Beast of Burden
You're No Good
Here's a Quarter, Call Someone Who Cares

Or Will I?!
Why Does Love Got to Be So Sad?
Lonesome Road
Another Piece of My Heart
I'll Never Fall in Love Again
I Keep Forgettin I Forgot About You
The Last Word in "Lonesome" Is "Me"
I Can't Make You Love Me
The complete works of Patsy Cline

I'm Not Bitter!
Who's That Girl?
Love Stinks
You're the Reason Our Kids Are Ugly
Don't You Mess Around with My Little Sister
The Smiths, A-Z

You'll Be Back!
Open Arms
Do You Really Want to Hurt Me?
Don't Give Up On Us
Against All Odds
Who's Gonna Mow Your Grass?

TWISTIN'...the Knife!
SHAKIN'...your head in disbelief!
MOVIN'...on!

The Breakup Was My Idea, But I'm Still Really Sad and Lonely Anyway!

Total Eclipse of the Heart
Always Something There to Remind Me
Sad Eyes
Biological Time Bomb

They Make You Cry, But You Don't Know Why!

The Rainbow Connection
Theme from St. Elmo's Fire
Home, Home on the Range

Songs with the Word "Tears" or "Cry" in the Title!

I've Got Tears in My Ears from Lyin on My Back Cryin Over You
If the Jukebox Took Teardrops, I'd Cry All Night Long
It's All Over But the Crying
Tracks of My Tears
All Cried Out

NOT!
Endless Love
Our House
My Baby Takes the Morning Train

Um, I Think Someone Needs to Talk to Your Friend!
Love Will Keep Us Together
Darling Be Home Soon
Wedding March from A Midsummer Night's Dream

SWEETS TO THE SOUR:

Finding Your Voice on

Valentine's Day

You don't need Breakup Girl to tell you that around, say, February 14 or so, you might feel, well, a little left out.

But you might need Breakup Girl to tell you that things don't have to be that way. It's time for Valentine's Day to include people from all walks of love: not only attached-Americans, but also the romantically-challenged, the differently-dating. And you can help make that difference. How? Convert to your own eleven-month pagan calendar? Spread a national rumor that longstem roses raise cholesterol?

Not necessary. We're working on a much smaller—indeed, bite-size—scale. We are talking about those bitter pills of pith, Valentine's conversation hearts. No wonder you feel

silenced: MY GUY and HOT STUFF—
not to mention FAR OUT and O U KID—
are not exactly the verbal tools you're looking
for on that special day.

The solution? Get out your fine-tipped non-
toxic laundry marker, and "Get me rewrite!"

That little heart might have entered its brief,
chalky life as TRY ME, but after a few quick pen
strokes on its flipside...

You now have the means to create
a love-lifetime supply of V-Day
dialogue. You can soften a blow:

harden your stance:

or give yourself some tender loving care:

(Some of you may choose to go ahead
and eat these little fellas. If so, a side of
garlic bread would be appropriate.)

The Low Blow of
HAIKU

When it comes to the poetry of misery, the lyrics of country music seem to have cornered the market: "The Last Word in Lonesome is 'Me,'" "...if my phone still ain't ringin', I assume it still ain't you"—it just doesn't get better—or worse—than that.

Or does it?

In the big picture, country music's stake in heartbreak is rather disingenuous. First of all, even the most morose words can be set to tunes that are downright toe-tappin'. Also, those singers are big stars. They have millions and millions of adoring fans (and, furthermore, are often happily married to their managers). Plus they get to appear in massive concerts and awards shows, with huge red hair, purple cowboy boots and chunky turquoise neck ornaments—all with complete impunity.

Really. How bad can things be?

For a much purer, bleaker form of self-expression during these troubled times, Breakup Girl suggests turning not to country-western, but to far-eastern Japan and the sparse, lonely, regimented verse of haiku. While country music bends the rules to allow even the most dubious rhymes, haiku, though unrhymed, has strict syllabic requirements that promise to constrain your creativity as much as your relationship did. Also, you will surely find some vexing hidden meaning in the syllable-count pattern of 5-7-5 (three digits that appear in his phone number, his height plus five inches, etc.).

Here, to get you started, are some haiku from Breakup Girl's personal notebook. Once you get the hang of it, you could consider inviting some friends over for a reading. (If you later become tempted to branch out into the ancient oral tradition of interminable, ponderous, heavily symbolic epic poetry, try to keep it to yourself.) And if you feel you must buy yourself some sequined cowboy boots for the occasion, go right ahead.

"It's not you," he said.
"Well, if it's 'not me,'" I said,
"Then dump someone else."

I hope he's happy.
Of course you realize that I'm
Being sarcastic.

Melodramatic!
It would be just like him to
Be writing haikus.

It's a matter of
What I want and what I don't
Want. Which are the same.

The night is so dark.
Dark, dark, it is dark as...night—
Oh, God, what's the point?

I guess I'm allowed
To see other people now.
But he sure isn't.

5 syllables **YOU CAN WRITE YOUR OWN**
7 syllables **JUST FOL LOW THIS DI A GRAM**
5 syllables **ITS EA SY AND FUN**

for later use
in case of
rebound

Heartbreak HOTEL

116

BREAKUP GIRL 🎩 **SUGGESTS...**

Good Movies To Rent

GOOD CRY:	*Bambi*
GOOD AND MAD:	*Bambi Meets Godzilla*
GOOD AND LONG:	*Gone with the Wind*
NOT A GOOD IDEA:	*A Little Romance*
	The Bridges of Madison County
	Betsy's Wedding
FEEL–GOOD:	*Muriel's Wedding*
GOOD BETS FOR AVOIDING LOVE SCENES:	*America's Funniest Sports Bloopers*
GOOD WOMEN:	*Thelma and Louise*
	Cannibal Women in the Avocado Jungle of Death
	anything with Mae West
GOOD GUYS:	*Benji*

He's so faithful...!

SEW YOUR OWN
VOODOO DOLL
(FROM BREAKUP GIRL'S HOME WRECKONOMICS CLASS)

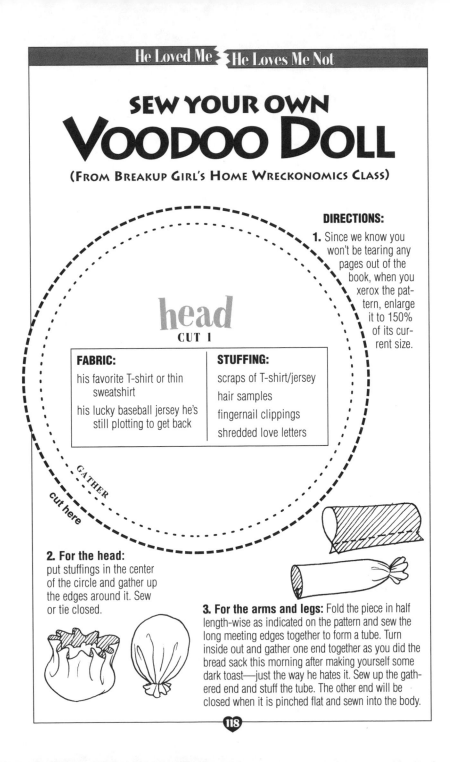

head
CUT 1

FABRIC:	STUFFING:
his favorite T-shirt or thin sweatshirt	scraps of T-shirt/jersey
	hair samples
his lucky baseball jersey he's still plotting to get back	fingernail clippings
	shredded love letters

GATHER

cut here

DIRECTIONS:

1. Since we know you won't be tearing any pages out of the book, when you xerox the pattern, enlarge it to 150% of its current size.

2. For the head: put stuffings in the center of the circle and gather up the edges around it. Sew or tie closed.

3. For the arms and legs: Fold the piece in half length-wise as indicated on the pattern and sew the long meeting edges together to form a tube. Turn inside out and gather one end together as you did the bread sack this morning after making yourself some dark toast—just the way he hates it. Sew up the gathered end and stuff the tube. The other end will be closed when it is pinched flat and sewn into the body.

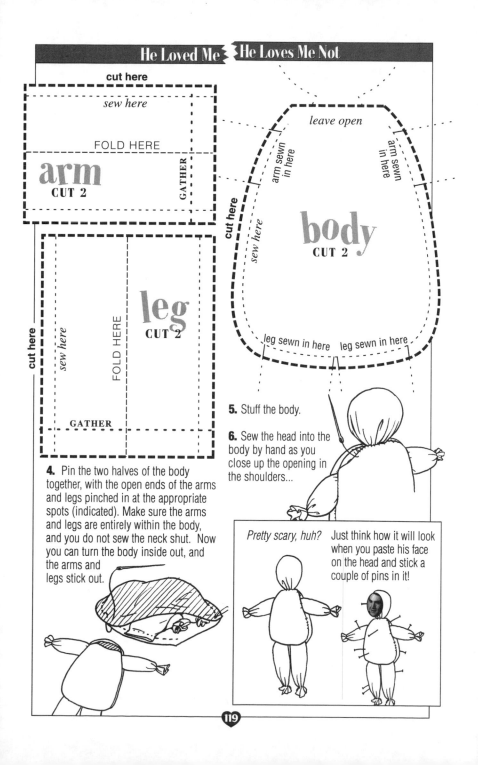

cut here

sew here

FOLD HERE

arm
CUT 2

GATHER

cut here

sew here

FOLD HERE

leg
CUT 2

GATHER

leave open

arm sewn in here

arm sewn in here

cut here

sew here

body
CUT 2

leg sewn in here   leg sewn in here

4. Pin the two halves of the body together, with the open ends of the arms and legs pinched in at the appropriate spots (indicated). Make sure the arms and legs are entirely within the body, and you do not sew the neck shut. Now you can turn the body inside out, and the arms and legs stick out.

5. Stuff the body.

6. Sew the head into the body by hand as you close up the opening in the shoulders...

Pretty scary, huh? Just think how it will look when you paste his face on the head and stick a couple of pins in it!

Breakup Central:
A Seek 'n' Find

The notion of "having your space" when you're in a relationship seems pretty darn cool, sensitive, mature. But when that relationship is over, "space" is beside the point. There's no one to have   from; it's all you have. Talk about *empty*.

But that's why your own room is going to become so important to you at this time. You should not just hang out there by default, wondering if there was always an echo, thinking how big and empty it is without his huge "#1" sports-fan glove. Instead, you need to reclaim that room as yours—as International Ouch-Potato Headquarters— where you are in charge. You need to set yourself up with everything you need to run the entire post-breakup operation-communication technology, provisions, personnel— without leaving your room (or if possible, your bed).

And just to kill time, we'll make it a game. Instructions: compare picture A (before the breakup) to Picture B (after), and try to find 14 items that are different between the two.

Answers to Seek'n'Find

In 2nd picture: **1.** flowers from "Mom," not "D.," **2.** door closed **3.** dart board as door accent **4.** only one tennis racket **5.** only one pair of in-line skates **6.** silk boxers replaced with flannel emporium catalog **7.** pottery wheel, equipment for impulsive new hobby (abandoned; excrutiating reminder of love scene in *Ghost*) **8.** radio in trash: only station that would come in was WCRY **9.** his "#1" sports-fan glove is outta there! **10.** art on wall now more closely imitates life **11.** occupant is home **12.** nightstand now fridge **13.** censured photo on nightstand **14.** BONUS: diaphragm, originally in nightstand drawer, now preserved cryogenically in freezer compartment

PICTURE A: BEFORE THE BREAKUP

PICTURE B: AFTER THE BREAKUP

BREAKUP GAME

Word Search

Here's a tricky mind-bender...and a fun way to review the concepts covered in the first two chapters. You may be searching for answers anyway, so you might as well search for the answers to the clues below in this grid (words run horizontally, vertically, and diagonally; backward and forward):

```
J  X  B  D  H  E  L  L  R  B  Y
E  U  A  I  G  O  A  T  E  E  K
A  W  S  S  U  N  U  N  M  P  H
L  B  M  T  T  R  J  J  A  V  A
O  V  A  A  F  I  C  M  R  U  P
U  Q  T  N  E  R  Z  O  C  H  Z
S  O  I  C  E  R  I  V  A  L  T
M  L  R  E  L  C  G  E  M  T  U
E  A  I  B  I  D  G  O  N  J  H
B  G  C  L  N  C  Y  N  P  D  C
L  H  E  Q  G  K  P  E  E  L  S
```

1. What you say if accused of being jealous. (_____? __?)

2. Person you're not jealous of

3. Point on the romance spectrum between lovers and mortal enemies

4. _____ of your existence

5. *Homo foetidus*

6. Facial hair as revenge

7. Facial blemish as revenge

8. Says "I love you" (hint: male, but not actual human)

9. Good guy (hint: male, but canine)

10. ___ West

11. Vower of chastity (by choice)

12. Your faithful companion (abbrev.)

13. Your faithful companion (liquid)

14. Your faithful companion (crustacean)

15. Breakup locale

16. Breakup pasttime

17. Breakup motivation: "It's just a ___ _____ "

18. _____ = RATE x TIME

19. Teddy bear murder weapon

20. Essential ingredient for first cooking project

21. Essential ingredient for shrewd, subtle revenge

22. "I'm ready to _____ __."

23. Famous last words: your solemn _____ that you will never date again

Word Search Answer Key

ZIGGY	GUT FEELING
ZIT	SLEEP
GOATEE	HELL
HIS B.O.	CRAB	OATH
BANE	JAVA	MOVE ON
JUST FRIENDS	TV	CHUTZPAH
(2 answers)	NUN	BASMATI RICE
HER and RIVAL	MAE	MACRAME
JEALOUS? ME?	BENJI	DISTANCE

BREAKUP ✏ QUIZ #2

1. Have you called a psychic hotline or "Jessica Hahn's Love Phone" within the past 24 hours?
2. Have you considered making your own potpourri?
3. Are you addicted to Tetris, Minesweeper, or Myst?
4. Have you reread anything by any Brontë sister?
5. Do you now own any of the following items: cheesecloth, a latch-hook, bread machine, *The Making of "Benji"*?

If you answered "yes" to three or more questions, continue on to Chapter Three. If not, buy a copy of *Martha Stewart's Living,* do at least three projects—even if it means embroidering your own tablecloth with thread made of the manes of wild Chincoteague ponies,weaving your own wallpaper out of dried hyacinths and Luxembourg lace, or breeding your own silkworms—and then try the quiz again.You're going to need all that stuff when the wedding storm hits, anyway.

THE CHANCE

MEETING

NUMBER TWO

WHERE:
the gym

Since when does he work out at 6:30 AM?! That must mean he went to bed pretty early, ha ha. Or else that he was with someone else who motivated him to get out of bed early because she had to be on the trading floor for the start of the Tokyo business day or something, oh God...

APPROPRIATE BODY LANGUAGE:
hands hang awkwardly at sides

APPROPRIATE THING TO SAY:

YOU: What's up?

HIM: Pretty good. How are you?

YOU: Not much.

CHAPTER THREE:
RENEWING YOUR COMMITMENT TO PERSONAL HYGIENE AND REENTERING SOCIETY

By this time,
for better or for worse,
your social life will start to pick up
by leaps and rebounds.

Here's how to deal.

Public Relations

At this point, your closest friends have so much information about the breakup that they could practically stand in for you on a detailed conversation with your ex, and no one would be the wiser. And they're not the only ones in the know: for that one 24-hour period, you spilled the whole story, from first date to final words, to anyone whose ear you could bend: the paper boy, Rolonda, the mysterious raven-haired stable hand.

But now you're going to have to deal with the other people: the ones with whom you aren't normally intimate but who will nonetheless badger you with highly personal

Nicole & Glenn's

BREAKUP AT-A-GLANCE

Answers to Frequently Asked Questions

Please refer to the following for information pertaining to "the deal" with Nicole and Glenn. Additional questions may be directed in writing to Nicole's mother at

70 Cary Avenue
St. Louis, MO 63103

or to
vicepresident@whitehouse.gov.

Q. But why? You guys were so cute.

A. Thanks, I know, it was just sort of, you know, a timing thing, a gut feeling kind of thing. You know, like time to move on. You know.

Q. Who broke up with who?

A. I guess it was pretty mutual.

and ultimately unanswerable questions, just when you're more than ready to drop the subject.

How to respond diplomatically?

DON'T say "I'm sorry, but I'd really rather not talk about it right now." The rumor mill will neatly, swiftly grind your evasion into an All-Points-Bulletin, "She's really bumming."

DO generate a point-by-point information management strategy. Implement your plan by devising a leaflet containing all necessary data. Carry copies with you, and distribute as necessary. (If you have the means, you may also want to consider creating an on-line FAQ file.)

3.
Q. Are you guys on okay terms?

A. Yeah, we're pretty civil, I guess. Is he here?

4.
Q. So now who are you going to take to Kim's, Eva's, Raquel's, Geoff's, Jake's, Emily's, Jenny's, Christina's, Doug's, and Adam's weddings?

A. Oh, I don't know, I haven't really figured that out yet.

5.
Q. Was there anyone else?

A. No, no, it wasn't that, it was just sort of, you know, a timing thing, a gut feeling kind of thing. You know, like time to move on. You know.

6.
Q. Oh, okay, so it had nothing to do with that thing with him and what's-her-name over at the mini-golf?

A. Huh?

Note: If he gets this idea from you, you may be able to get some of your questions answered.

GLENN AND NICOLE'S
BREAKUP-AT-A-GLANCE:
Answers to Frequently Asked Questions

Please refer to the following for information pertaining to "the deal" with Glenn and Nicole. Additional questions may be directed to andrewdiceclay@dorknet.com.

1. Q. But why? You guys were so cute.
   A. Thanks, I know, it was just sort of, you know, a timing thing, a gut feeling kind of thing. You know, like time to move on. You know.

2. Q. Did you break up with her?
   A. Yeah. I did.

3. Q. Are you guys on okay terms?
   A. Yeah, I guess. She keeps calling me.

4. Q. So now who are you going to take to Kim's, Eva's, Raquel's, Geoff's, Jake's, Emily's, Jenny's, Christina's, Doug's, and Adam's weddings?
   A. Oh, I don't know, maybe I'll meet someone.

5. Q. Was there anyone else?
   A. I can't believe you'd even *ask* that, man.

6. Q. Wanna go play mini-golf again tonight?
   A. Yeah, sure.

Party POLITICS

S ome of the more brutal breakups can split a group of friends into his-and-hers factions, complete with turf wars, gang colors, and the like. But even after a rumble or two, sooner or later, your mutual friends will attempt to move on with their lives. And that means a call to arms for a one-on-one turf war of your very own:

when you're both invited to the same party.

Should you go? Of course. You don't want him to think you're running scared. Remember, you have access to higher powers: radar, supersonic hearing, and X-ray vision. These will allow you to give your full attention to a discussion of First Amendment Theory or "Land of the Lost" trivia out on the porch, and be fully aware at all times of where he is, whom he's talking to, and who's checking him out.*

For tracking purposes, those skills are invaluable. But some situations may require actual intervention.

For example...

---

* Scientists have identified such party situations as early omniscience-training for motherhood.

EMERGENCY MEASURES

SITUATION: He's been talking with that woman by the food table for ten minutes.

ACTION: Have someone create a diversion (example: put on retro hit such as "Y.M.C.A." or "Rock Lobster." Any guests who do not proceed immediately to perform corresponding interpretive dance will at least be distracted by being studiously cooler than those who do). Now, replace yogurt dip with onion dip.

ONION DIP

EMERGENCY MEASURES

SITUATION: He's been talking with that woman by the food table for twenty minutes.

ACTION: Do a sweep of the house, concealing all visible writing implements (including eyeliners). If he wants to get the digits, he's going to have to work for them.

SITUATION: He's been talking with that woman for nearly half an hour. You've seen enough. Still, you must leave on the moral/social high ground.

ACTION: Have a friend call you at the party from a nearby pay phone. When you answer, state the following loudly and clearly: "Cool, I'll head right over. Just help me keep all the Kennedys' names straight, will ya?" Depart quickly, yet graciously.

"It's My Party"

...Throw Your Own

It's important for you to be back out on the circuit at this time, to see and be seen, to scope and be scoped, to actually have a pretty good time and then cry all the way home in a cab. But you, the gracious guest, might also wish to try your hand at hostessing. That way, you'll have control of the guest list, the menu—and whom you go home with. Here are some of Breakup Girl's favorite recovery party themes:

THE SLIMIES
An Awards Banquet
Host a gala event for the girls. Present awards for: Best Actor, Least Supportive, Most Memorable Score, etc.

TECHNICAL ACHIEVEMENT

The After-Prom Party
When: 1 AM
Wear: formal/disheveled
What: Drink beer purchased by someone older; hook up with someone else's date

An Anti-Shower

Make a grab-bag of gifts that are not cute, sexy, or at all useful in any room of the home.

A 50s Hors D'oeuvres Party

A potluck of marshmallow-and-mandarin-orange kabobs, spam-and-pineapple pinwheels, etc. You may not be married now, but at least you weren't married then.

A 70s Party

...to honor the time when you dressed like that and people went out with you anyway.

BREAKUP JOKES

Q. How many ex-girlfriends does it take to screw in a lightbulb?

A. I'm lonely enough; please don't say *screw*.

Q. How many ex-boyfriends does it take to change a lightbulb?

A. *Change? **Him?***

Q. Why did the ex-boyfriend cross the road?

A. I don't know why, but I can tell you where, when, and whom he was with.

Q. Why are all breakup jokes one-liners?

A. Because that's all ex-girlfriends have time for in their busy social schedules.

A Harvard guy, a Princeton guy, and a Yale guy are walking in the desert. All of a sudden, they run into my mother, who gives them my phone number.

No, wait, that was a nightmare.

The Relapse

or—With "Friends" Like These, Who Needs Boyfriends?

SAM: "I hate you!"
DIANE: "I hate you!"
SAM: "Are you as horny as I am?"
DIANE: "More!"

There's no aphrodisiac like animosity.

You make plans to stop by that one last time to pick up that one last pair of sneakers. Get the footwear home, you say to yourself, and you'll finally have some sense of closure.

But when you both kneel down and reach into the closet at the same time, your hands brush each other's, and bam!—there's more than footwear on the floor.

Twenty minutes later, rug-burned but rewarded, it's like you never hated each other. What does this mean? Was it all a mistake? Is that a sneaker digging into your left shoulder blade?

There's only one thing to do at a time like this: rationalize.

It's just like when you cheat on a diet. All is not lost; you just had a little moment of spontaneous, guilty pleasure (and besides, you had it with a diet soda). Some additional parallels:

> "I like rationalizing more than sex, which is why I do it more often."
> — *Woody Allen*

DIET-LAPSE
RATIONALIZATION

It was dark

It was only half

It was free

I don't even like cheesecake

I ate it standing up

RELAPSE
RATIONALIZATION

It was daytime

It was only once

I got my sneakers back

I don't even like him

We weren't actually in bed

Someone Blue:

Other People's Weddings

In an odd way, the first few weeks after a breakup may, socially speaking, be your busiest ever. Your friends will bombard you with phone calls and plans "just to get your mind off things"—why, you'll be a regular butterfly.

The actual life span of a butterfly, however, is only about a month. Soon enough, the initial crisis-mode flutter starts to die down. Does that mean you're headed straight for a lonely spell of pay-per-view and cooking-for-one?

Hardly. Oh, you'll be plenty busy.

And why is that?

Annex your mailbox and polish your pumps, girlfriend, because it's time for *other people's weddings*.

Somehow, it seems, your breakup has released into the air a pungent pheromone that, upon contact with other couples, causes marriage. Not since college-admissions April have you been so acutely envelope-conscious. Back then, the mail check (hourly) hinged on thick versus thin;

140

now, the mail check (weekly) hinges on "occupant" versus calligraphy. That telltale fountain pen script will tip you off not only to weddings themselves, but also to other nuptial nuisances: engagement toasts, rehearsal dinners, bridal teas, and showers with darling themes that turn gift shopping into a scavenger hunt.

The wedding epidemic, for that matter, is not confined only to the events you're invited to. It can spread to any newspaper you touch (especially the *New York Times*, where everyone getting married also has a cooler job than you), to any alumni magazine you pick up, and even to the phone lines, where every conversation with your mother includes the news of someone else's vows. ("How about vows of silence?" you may wish to ask.)

Mind you, this presumption of bitterness doesn't necessarily have anything to do with some outmoded idea that ring-digging is your full-time job, that your biological clock is set to Marriage Mean Time, or that you're incomplete without someone else's last name.

No, no, no—it's just that it's all such a *hassle.* You've invested so much time in getting to know one another, learning about give and take, reaching the point where you could sit on the toilet while he brushed his teeth, and now, dammit—assuming you meet someone else—you've got to start all over again.

This could take *years,* for goodness sake.

In the meantime, you may regard this wedding spree as a fulfilling, expedient learning experience. When your time comes, heck, you'll already know all there is to know about pulling off the big event. No need to buy "Your Special Day" software, nor to take that day-long workshop at the Y. You will be the *alpha-bride.* You will already have developed a casual fluency with terms such as "alphabet shower," "nosegay," and "snood;" a

Gee, Lynn— this is a lotta text! You're not bitter, are ya?

sharp eye for great little dresses that your bridesmaids can wear again; and an educated opinion on the buffet vs. sit-down debate.

(Alternatively, by the time your time comes, all weddings will take place in virtual reality. This technological advance will render unnecessary such logistics as hotel rooms, ushers, and flower arrangements, and will thus cut your to-do list way down. TIP: VR helmets may also do double duty as bridesmaids' gifts.)

And even if your time never does come, at least you can write a column.

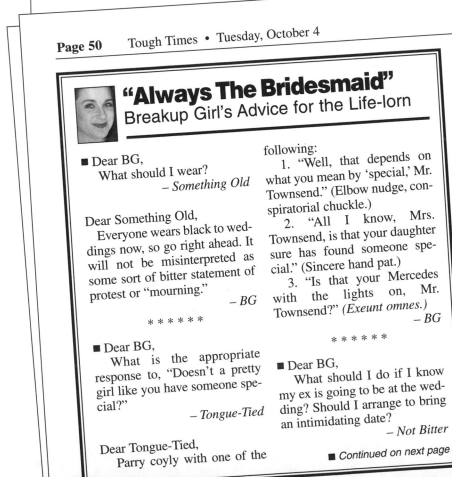

"Always The Bridesmaid"
Breakup Girl's Advice for the Life-lorn

■ Dear BG,
   What should I wear?
               – *Something Old*

Dear Something Old,
   Everyone wears black to weddings now, so go right ahead. It will not be misinterpreted as some sort of bitter statement of protest or "mourning."
               – *BG*

* * * * * *

■ Dear BG,
   What is the appropriate response to, "Doesn't a pretty girl like you have someone special?"
               – *Tongue-Tied*

Dear Tongue-Tied,
   Parry coyly with one of the

following:
   1. "Well, that depends on what you mean by 'special,' Mr. Townsend." (Elbow nudge, conspiratorial chuckle.)
   2. "All I know, Mrs. Townsend, is that your daughter sure has found someone special." (Sincere hand pat.)
   3. "Is that your Mercedes with the lights on, Mr. Townsend?" *(Exeunt omnes.)*
               – *BG*

* * * * * *

■ Dear BG,
   What should I do if I know my ex is going to be at the wedding? Should I arrange to bring an intimidating date?
               – *Not Bitter*

■ *Continued on next page*

"Always The Bridesmaid"
■ *Continued from previous page*

Dear Not Bitter,

Oh, no. Certainly not. That would be contrived, bordering on tacky. Instead, purchase an actual engagement ring (be sure to keep the receipt), or persuade someone to lend you one by offering to mow their lawn. If someone asks you why your fiance couldn't make it, smile mysteriously and murmur words such as "yacht" or "Onassis" into your drink.

– BG

* * * * * *

■ Dear BG,

They're trying to fix me up with the best man, who is anything but. In fact, I wouldn't go out with him if he were the last best man on earth. What should I do?

– Maid of Dishonor

Dear Maid,

Inform "best" that "Daddy" has already "arranged" for you to catch the bouquet. And "Daddy," you'll say, will be "very unhappy" if "best" does not, in turn, catch the garter— which "means" that *you two will be the next to be engaged!* He'll leave you alone.

– BG

■ Dear BG,

What if I am the only "single girl" who lines up to catch the bouquet?

– Hot Potato

Dear Hot,

Throw it back.

– BG

* * * * * *

■ Dear BG,

I know I'm a "bridesmaid," but what do you call married bridal attendants?

– Heinous Dress

Dear Dress,

"Matrons." Ha, ha.

–BG

* * * * * *

■ Dear BG,

Will my friends start to forget about me as they get on with their married lives?

– Maiden Aunt

Dear Aunt,

Not at all. In time, you'll come to be their kids' favorite grownup friend, as in "Mom, don't . forget to ask 'Auntie' Margie to come to the pageant!" or "Well, maybe 'Auntie' Margie can drive us. She's usually not doing anything."

– BG

How Your Mother Will React

1 Every time you mention where you're going, she will analyze your destination for its matchmaking potential. For her analysis, she will use a chart such as this:

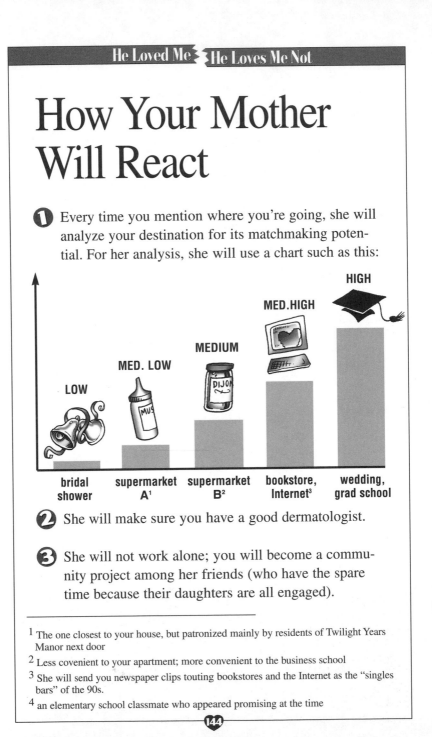

2 She will make sure you have a good dermatologist.

3 She will not work alone; you will become a community project among her friends (who have the spare time because their daughters are all engaged).

---

1 The one closest to your house, but patronized mainly by residents of Twilight Years Manor next door

2 Less covenient to your apartment; more convenient to the business school

3 She will send you newspaper clips touting bookstores and the Internet as the "singles bars" of the 90s.

4 an elementary school classmate who appeared promising at the time

4 She will reinstate your clothing allowance to insure that you will "look nice" at all times. (When she informs you of her intention, you will [a] say, "Mom, I really don't think that's necessary," and [b] accept.)

5 She will ask "Whatever happened to _____?"[4]

6 She will request clarification about any male name you mention in conversation ...

When Your Friends Get Boyfriends

As the dust continues to settle, you will start to notice that when it comes to relationships, your friends fall into roughly two categories: (A) those who are more jaded than you are, and (B) those who regard you, with some degree of awe, as the wise, all-knowing One Who Has Been There. They will come to you for guidance, saying that they never realized how little they knew about relation-ships. (Concurrently, as you listen and advise, you will come to realize that you now know so much about rela-tionships that you really don't need to have any more.)

This, too, shall pass. After all, category B is often merely a stepping-stone to category A. Bear in mind, also, that the level of detail you have to endure in your friends' discourse is inversely proportional to the length of time they've been seeing the person in question. To illustrate:

11:20 AM

Hi, it's me. If you're there pick up. Oh my god I am dying. Are you there? I have got to talk to you. Call me as soon as you get this. I have to tell you about last night, I had the best time, we talked until literally like five hours ago. And that was when we'd been together since like ten, well, I met him at Grendel's at 10:07, you know, not too late, not too on-time, and good call on the shoes, by the way, the floor there is kind of sawdusty, and if I'd worn those mules like I was talking about I would have gotten all sorts of grit in them and it would have been a total pain, so okay, anyway, so I see him before he sees me because he's looking at the bar menu, only I think he was kind of looking up for me too, only cool, like not looking around desperately, just mellow. So I go "hi" and he goes "hi" and we both kind of laugh, which was cool, like acknowledging that it was awkward, you know, our first date and everything, but not like anything majorly weird. So I sit down and he goes "How are you?" asking about me first, like how often does that happen? So of course I say something lame like "Fine thanks, how are you?" but luckily the waitress comes right then and asks what we wanted to drink and I wait to see what he orders so I can get something similar, so he'd think I had good taste but it wasn't like I was just copying him—I am so lame, I can't believe I still do stuff like that—but anyway then he goes, "Do you like calamari?" and I'm like cool, he likes food, he's not weirded out by squid or whatever, and I go, "Yeah, I love it," and I'm psyched, but of course I'm panicked because it comes with red sauce and I'm so sure I'm going to get some on my shirt and then have to put water on it and totally look like I'm lactating or something, but anyway...

...So we're still sitting there talking while they're sweeping and stacking the chairs on the tables and stuff, and they practically have to kick us out of the place, so we leave and just start walking and keep talking...

...and so we're talking over by the bridge for, I swear to God, like three hours, I don't even know what we're talking about, but it just flows, I don't have to like act interested or try to think of things to say or anything...

...so when he drops me off, I swear to God the birds are already starting to chirp and we're like "okay, we totally have to go." And the cutest thing is that I look and I notice that he has like a little red sauce spot on his shirt, which is like the cutest thing in the world, like he's totally human and fallible and stuff. And of course I totally want him to come up, but I totally don't because that tension and expectation is so cool and everything, and I totally know there'll be a next time because he gives me this kiss on the cheek, like totally not one of those polite "I'll call you..NOT" kisses, but like the real thing, like with some pressure, and it lasted like six seconds, and I turned my head toward him a little, so it was a little closer to my lips than maybe he'd planned, but still totally not like a real lip kiss, but at least I think he got the message that I wanted him to and stuff. Oh my god, I'm dying...

...so call me call me call me so I can give you the details!

☎☎☎☎
11:45 AM
Hi, it's me. I was just thinking, is it still a bad time for you for stuff like this?

☎☎☎☎
Three Weeks Later
...so what do you think his deal is?

fwd

Five Months Later
Call me call me call me, I know I haven't talked to you about this much and it might seem sudden, but we might be moving in together...!

OR

Five Months Later
Um, do you still have that book, *He Loved Me, He Loves Me Not*?

☎☎☎☎

Anatomy of a Rebound

You've heard of beer goggles––now try *breakup* goggles. But first, complete the following worksheet to ensure that you are in the rebound situation that is right for you.
Check one answer in each group.

1. The situation should fit one of the following categories:

   a) *"I'm only in town for one night."* A fling with some-one so inappropriate that he unleashes your wildest passions while remaining harmless and inconsequen-tial (e.g., the mysterious raven-haired stable hand; the Basque terrorist in the U.S. for a 2-day pavement kayaking tournament; Richard Simmons)

   b) *"I Came in at 2 with a 10 and Woke Up at 10 with a 2."* A shameful, regrettable episode that will cause you to shudder/shower frequently for weeks to come

   c) *"Uh, hi."* Choose one:
      - the guy in the next cube
      - the guy in the next room
      - your ex-boyfriend's best friend
      - your best friend's ex-boyfriend
      - your little sister's boyfriend
      - your ex-boyfriend's stepfather

2. He must be someone you
   a) just met
   b) always knew you'd hook up with
   c) swore you'd never hook up with

3. You met him
   a) at your high-school or college reunion
   b) at a bar in another state
   c) at a Monster Truck show
   d) while haggling over the house phone bill
   e) at your ex's apartment

Been THERE, done HIM

4. He must be someone

    a) your mother would love, but he puts you to sleep

    b) you love, but he would put your mother on the phone to the police

---

Checklist to assist you with #4
Select choice (a) if he has:
   – a calendar or watch
   – a steady job
   – a car*
   – a clean shave
   – library card
   – utensils

Select choice (b) if he has:
   – a goatee
   – a goat
   – a 2–week old ink stamp on the back of his hand
   – a tattoo
   – a tattoo parlor

---

5. For the episode, you must wear

    a) something your ex–boyfriend gave you

    b) something your ex-boyfriend wants back

    c) patent leather pumps, official footwear of the sunrise Walk of Shame

---

*but if he lives in a van, check (b).

BREAKUP GAME

Cute Couple Bingo

◆ Get a single friend to be your bingo partner (ask around, you'll find one).

◆ Fill in the empty grids provided with names or photos of cute couples you know, making sure that the grids do not match one another.

◆ Every time one of the depicted couples makes their cute presence known (e.g., borrowing the heart-shaped waffle iron your great aunt gave you, sending pre-printed Christmas cards, asking you to take care of their joint cat while they're at the bed & breakfast) mark their space with a Sweet Tart or Tiddly Wink (or simply blacken in the space with a big fat permanent marker).

◆ First to get five in a row wins!

Cute Couple Bingo

Cute Couple Bingo

BREAKUP QUIZ #3

Do you now have (check all that apply):

☐ a brave new haircut?

☐ or at least a great hat?

☐ your sneakers back?

☐ a good dermatologist?

☐ a "good" suit?

☐ a "wedding" dress?

☐ a system for stocking up on wedding and shower gifts ahead of time?

☐ friends who've stopped *not* mentioning their boyfriends around you?

☐ already only a dim memory of a hook-up that had been waiting to happen?

If you checked six or more, move on to Chapter Four. If not, tell your mother you need a raise.

THE CHANCE

MEETING

NUMBER THREE

WHERE:
mutual friends' wedding

APPROPRIATE BODY LANGUAGE:
limp hand clasp, then choppy air-kiss (just one side,
unless he went to Europe to try to forget you, in which
case, left *and* right)

**APPROPRIATE
THING TO SAY:**

Table 6? Oh, no, mine's
actually a 9.

CHAPTER FOUR:
BEYOND THE REBOUND: MOVING ON

Being a mature grownup,
you can now assert that the whole episode
was a valuable learning experience.

You have learned about
what you want in a boyfriend
(a car),
and what you don't want
(a boyfriend, if it means
having to go through
all this again).

How to *Meet*

orget about singles events and set-ups*. It's not going to happen when you're planning on it. Your best bet is to frequent unlikely places (tollbooths, carnival sideshows, your ex's apartment), unprepared (wearing sweats, tinted zit cream, a shower cap, and your third-to-last pair of glasses with a big toothpaste smudge on the lens). There's more to this reasoning than the simple adage "expect the unexpected." Why?

Tempus fugit. You no longer have the time or patience to guide a new guy gently through the trusting, intimate archaeological excavation that will gradually reveal, under layers of borrowed clothing and Subdermal Hydrating Alpha-

SE

TURN OFF ENGINE

---

* but don't rule out the personals. See p. 162.

156

People

Hydroxy Humectant Liposome Collagen Système, a gal who naturally habitates boxers and a sports bra and who tends to be considerably less perky in real life than she is in "Meet Other Single Professionals" mode. If he can't take it, you're outta there. However, the guy who'll chat with you at the gas station while you're self-serve squeegeeing, wearing a muumuu and flipflops, with an entire chicken wing stuck in your teeth, is a guy who wants to get to know *you.* (The only drawback is the possibility that he'll be drawn to you because he's wearing a similar outfit.)

How to **Meet People**

"Your father..."

Here's another reason to look beyond the bars. If you're going to settle down, you've got to have a *good story*. Imagine this conversation with a hopeful, dreamy child:

CHILD: Mommy, how did you meet Daddy?

YOU: At an event for single people to meet one another.

CHILD: Oh.

Wouldn't you rather have that exchange go something like this:

CHILD: Mommy, how did you meet Daddy?

YOU: Well, honey, Mommy used to be a princess and also an astronaut. One day at the royal space station, I was at an event for single people to meet one another, and I spilled my drink on a very nice-looking man. I was so embarrassed! I offered to get his shirt cleaned for him, but instead he just said, "If you'll take a ride with me on my magic unicorn, we'll just forget about the whole thing." Well, off I went. And do you know what? That man was your father.

CHILD: Wow! I love you, Mommy.

Now, it is possible that you've never held high ranking in, say, a local kingdom or aeronautics project. No problem—all around you are great stories waiting to happen. While your single friends are getting their hair done for their video dating service screen tests, focus your attention instead on getting yourself into your share of great-story-producing situations. Use the list below for inspiration; your future family will thank you. And think of all the errands you'll get done.

▶ TRY HANGING OUT IN/AT:

Sun.	Mon.	Tues.	Wed.	Thurs.	Fri.	Sat.
the kennel	Department of Motor Vehicles	the chimney sweep's	exterminator's office	hardware store	dressing room (Big 'n' Old dept.)	cock fight

A TIP FROM BREAKUP GIRL

If you're standing in line at the DMV or watching the shark tank week after week, yet sparking few conversations, it may be time to bring out the Secret Weapon. It's the one item on the planet that is universally guaranteed to draw people over to you, to make you completely, absolutely magnetic. No one has the power to resist. Light, easy to carry with you at all times, *it's bubble paper*. Get some now and watch your social life start poppin'!

Meeting People On-Line:

Listen to Your Mother

*Surely, at some point, your mother
must have said something like:*

"Whatever you do, don't pick up anyone along the highway."

She could never have imagined that this warning might someday apply to the "highway" built by those phone lines that plug into your computer—but she's onto something. For many people, on-line dating services or chat-room minglings are the heaven-sent solution to problems of shyness, lack of car, etc. But do you ever feel a tad sneaky, or a bit, well, *bad,* as you hunt-and-peck for that spark ? It may be because, in effect, your mother is watching. Though her bytes of wisdom certainly predate the modem, eerily, clairvoyantly, somehow they seem to apply...

"You don't know where that's been."

Meeting someone. While the anonymity of the 'net is a haven for some, it also means that for all you know, you could actually be corresponding with a 13-year-old boy, a 65-year-old man, an

FBI agent, or, God forbid, a reporter. Furthermore, when you chat with someone on the Internet, you are, in a sense, on-line with everyone else he's ever been on-line with. How do you know, for example, if he's been tested for Carpal Tunnel Syndrome?

"Don't sit too close."

Liking someone. An Internet address gives him a whole nother way not to call you. Waiting by the computer is not only lamer than waiting by the phone, but according to the newspaper clippings your mother has sent you, those electro-magnetic rays emitted by your computer, clock radio, television, and microwave, will kill you, make you infertile, or at least make your glasses prescription thicker, thereby rendering the whole meeting-someone enterprise pointless to begin with.

"You'll freeze that way."

Really liking someone. So let's say you're getting into some heavy instant-messaging. You're describing your best cyber-hickey (The best kind! No turtlenecks!) in your best purple prose, when all of a sudden—crash!—your screen is paralyzed. Frozen. The cursor is dead to the world, but your live conversation beautifully preserved. Guaranteed, it is at this moment that your housemate or boss will peek over your shoulder to see how you're doing at Mortal Kombat.

Or is that your mother's phantom-like reflection in your screen...?

the
Personal Ad *and You*

Entering the world of placing and answering personal ads may actually have a calming effect on the otherwise turbulent seas of post-breakup dating. Why? Because here, for once, you know what to expect.

How could that be, you ask, when all you have to go on are three lines of text, and suspect text at that? It's because, at some level, the date is indeed consistent with the ad. Perhaps not in actual content, no—that is, "attractive" may turn out to mean "avid magnet collector"—but at some more fundamental level. In other words, you pretty much have a guarantee that the date, like the ad, will be composed of sentence-fragments, half truths, and morsels (comestible or factual) embellished to mask blandness. So there you have it. You know exactly what you're in for.

> **Note:** There is one case in which personal ads may tell the absolute truth. When someone is compelled to specify that he has a "sense" of humor, he clearly has just that: a *sense* of humor. Not a "grasp" of humor, and certainly not a "mastery," bless his heart, but simply a "sense." Like a "sense," for example, of when to laugh while viewing *Weekend at Bernie's II*. Otherwise, don't expect much.

POINTERS FOR:

Writing a Personal Ad

Too broad

SF seeks male carbon-based life form, bipeds preferred. Pulse a must.

Too specific

SF seeks SM, 5' 11," brown hair, hazel eyes (more on the green side when you wear that old gray sweatshirt). I enjoy film noir, spicy food, Dylan, mountain biking, *The X-Files*. Thought you did too. What's your problem, anyway?

BREAKUP GIRL PRESENTS

CONSUMER AFFAIRS...

It worked for *Jurassic Park*, now let it work for you. Remember that the word "advertisement" is central to the term "personal ad." If you have the financial means and the access to the proper product licensing channels, why sell yourself short with dime-a-dozen lines of black-and-white text? You could consider a much more elaborate campaign based on novelties like:

"You've got the doll...now how about a date? It's the Annie B. **Lookin-for-Action** *Figure!"*

"ABC gum—Already Been Chewed-up-and-Spit-Out! Bubbly, sweet, in search of someone who won't walk all over me!"

the Personal Ad AND You

Interpreting a Personal Ad

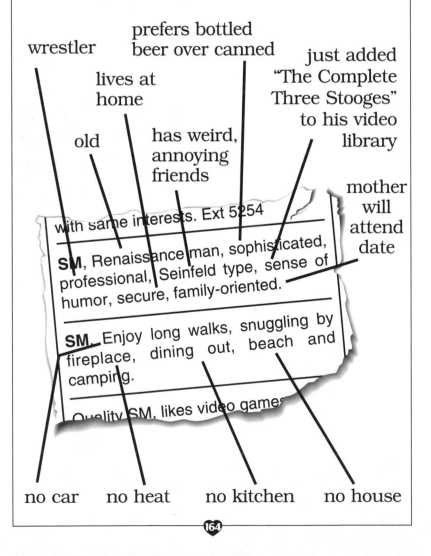

wrestler

prefers bottled beer over canned

just added "The Complete Three Stooges" to his video library

lives at home

old

has weird, annoying friends

mother will attend date

with same interests. Ext 5254

SM, Renaissance man, sophisticated, professional, Seinfeld type, sense of humor, secure, family-oriented.

SM. Enjoy long walks, snuggling by fireplace, dining out, beach and camping.

Quality SM, likes video games

no car   no heat   no kitchen   no house

the Personal Ad *and You*

Answering a Personal Ad

A. Do not answer any ad that:

- ▶ refers to potential mate as "Lady"
- ▶ states that act of placing ad indicates that SM is "ready to love again"
- ▶ contains the word "nice"
- ▶ contains Disney imagery
- ▶ describes placer of ad as "well-groomed"
- ▶ specifies "no MSG"
- ▶ resembles the following:

"SM, attractive, sensitive, intelligent, sense of humor, enjoys candlelight dinners, good conversation, walks on beach, cuddling, seeks slim, pretty SF for fun, friendship, maybe more...?!"

Note: This stipulation will eliminate 90-95% of all personal ads.

B. Most ads these days include the number of a voice mail box. The cost of responding to such ads is approximately $5,806.99 per minute.

YOU CAN CUT DOWN ON THESE CHARGES BY CALLING IN TO HEAR THE PERSON'S OUTGOING MESSAGE AND THEN HANGING UP PROMPTLY WHEN YOU HEAR THE BEEP.

Going on the Date

There are, ultimately, only four basic outcomes.

CLOSE

You perform a weekly ritual of circling the ads that look promising, and then moving on to your horoscope (which, dependably, says things like "fun, friendship, maybe more not in your stars this week" and "Be wary of strangers who claim to be 'Ivy-educated'").

CLOSER

You notice the safety guidelines in the personals section of the newspaper or magazine: "Be sure to meet in a crowded, well-lit place." You realize that the only such places you can think of are (a) your college library, and (b) your own bathroom.

...BUT NO CIGAR

You communicate with "SM" only through voice mail and arrange to meet in a cafe that is a safe distance from the stomping grounds of everyone you know ("They make great biscotti at this little place right over the state line!"). "SM," it turns out, is perhaps better described as "ET," not only because he's really short, but also because he keeps getting up, inexplicably, to use the phone.

CLOSE CALL!

You communicate with "SM" only through voice mail and arrange to meet in a cafe that is a safe distance from the stomping grounds of everyone you know. You spot him before he sees you and realize you know him from high school.

Your First Post-Him Date

You meet at a trendy bistro where you're both posing as regulars. Over foccaccia and olive paste, you appear deeply absorbed in the college name game. "Hmm, yeah, oh, that totally sounds familiar—crew team, right? Wait, Glee Club."

But you know what? You're not even really talking to this guy at all. You're dealing directly with the little cartoon guys perched on each of his shoulders. Right shoulder, your ex; left, your date in 5 to 10 years. Plus there's the whole cast of characters hovering around behind him—your parents, your clergyperson, a vaguely formed baby with "your eyes" and "his chin"—like some Spielberg/PBS mélange of *A Christmas Carol, Macbeth,* and *Who Framed Roger Rabbit?* Why this trippy tableau? Because it's too late for a frivolous rebound, yet too soon to treat anyone as an actual human. Throughout this date, you will parlay everything your earnest prix-fixe partner says or does into either a reminder of or comparison to "how things were," or a clue as to what it would be like to be together forever. So basically, let's just hope bistro-man has some major hidden flaw (pyromania, ties to skinhead groups, liked *The Bridges of Madison County*) because he could be a Rhodes scholar/J. Crew model/triathlete/school volunteer/heir to the M&M-Mars fortune who enjoys baking bread and building his own furniture...but with you, right here, right now, he does not stand a chance.

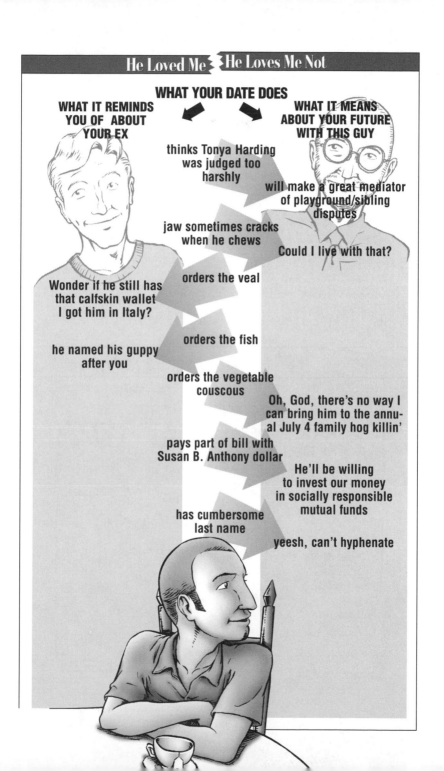

Bad Signs

Learning from our mistakes is an essential survival skill. Yet we are much better students in some situations *("OW! Orange stove burner hot!...Do not touch again!")* than we are in others *("OW! Man on motorcycle unreliable!...Date again!")*. Here are some warning signs that will help you get out of the kitchen while you still can.

WHEN YOU go to his house for the first time...

What's on Your Laptop?

Kelly Greene, before the breakup

Hooray!
e-mail
from
John!

Kelly Greene, after the breakup

Before the breakup	After the breakup
list of gift ideas for his birthday, other upcoming holidays list of	housewares I need for my room (sheets, door), now that I actually live there
my schedule	my living will
calendar of our anniversaries (by month)	{system error message}
data base of his family members' addresses for Christmas, birthday cards	data base of 3rd-year students at local law schools with jobs lined up for next year, scored by hacker friend
his resume	his resume, with "detail-oriented" spelled wrong
draft of my novel	alt.erotica.womyn
draft of guest list	draft of pre-dating agreement, for "next time"
list of restaurants we've been meaning to go to	map illustrating territorial settlements (see "There Goes the Neighborhood," p. 46)
interactive CD-ROM	Solitaire

I suppose
my lap isn't
good enough for
you either...!?

What's on his Laptop?

some weird virus...!?

THE PLAY SCALE:

Your First Post-Him Sexual Encounter

We're not talking about rebounds here: those are just blips, love in a vacuum, mere detours (if not dead ends). Believe it or not, sooner or later you will find yourself thinking about going the distance with someone—saints be praised!—who just may be an actual pin on the map of romance.

For some of the still-smarting, this may wind up being only a near-bed experience. When things heat up, you get the chills. You will be a bundle of nerves, as supple and yielding as the Statue of Liberty. Say hello to moving-on-us interruptus. "I can't go through with this," you think. "It's too soon...I'm too tired to suck in my stomach...I'm too old to be leaving my contact lenses in shot glasses...What if I cry out 'Oh, Pooky!?' No way." File that away under "At Least Someone Found Me Attractive Again," and give yourself a little more time.

Many of you, however, will be ready—really ready— to jump in. (If you're really really really ready, see below.) Now, advocates of safe sex warn you, soberingly enough, that when you sleep with someone, you "sleep with everyone else they've slept with." Well. Advocates of post-breakup sex would like to warn you that when you sleep with someone, you sleep with everyone else *you've* slept with. Here's how it works:

Your past sex life	Means next time will be	Because
Ex was great in bed	→ Great	You owe your ex for your sexual awakening
	↘ Awful	No one will ever make you feel the way your ex did
Ex was awful in bed	→ Great	New guy was at least *in the room*
	↘ Awful	Your ex caused you to lose all interest

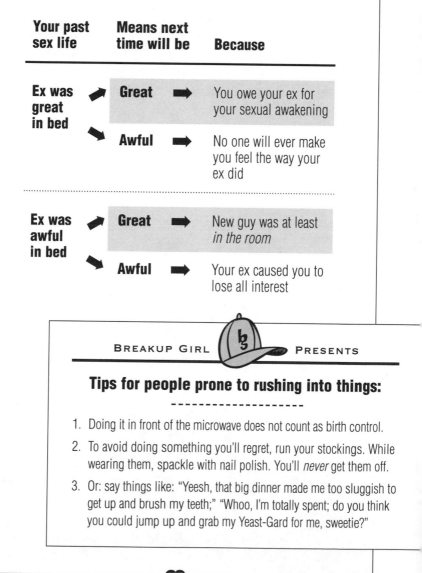

BREAKUP GIRL PRESENTS

Tips for people prone to rushing into things:

1. Doing it in front of the microwave does not count as birth control.

2. To avoid doing something you'll regret, run your stockings. While wearing them, spackle with nail polish. You'll *never* get them off.

3. Or: say things like: "Yeesh, that big dinner made me too sluggish to get up and brush my teeth;" "Whoo, I'm totally spent; do you think you could jump up and grab my Yeast-Gard for me, sweetie?"

His First Post-You Date

You generally pride yourself on your omniscience. However, you will hear about this development from the local gossip, who "thought you already knew." Remember, the grapevine does not discriminate. Its defamatory tendrils coil in both directions. That means you're going to have to play it cool as you dig for more dirt. Your detective work must be subtle, hands-off, coolly rooted in human psychology.

aerobics instructor

someone who looks exactly like you

a Fulbright scholar

someone who's your exact opposite

the gossip herself

Do not say: "<u>Who</u> <u>is</u> <u>she</u>?! I hope they know they're both making a big mistake. What are her weak points, vulnerabilities? Any phobias, international secrets, serious allergies...? If you can provide me with any information, I shall reward your efforts handsomely, my friend!"

Do say: "Oh, yeah, I did hear something about that," and go back to your crossword puzzle. Your bluff is guaranteed to get that gossip's goat. Once you get her talking, you'll be able to start to create a composite of the suspect, who is likely to fit the description of one of these shady characters:

a model

a waitress working the graveyard shift in order to swing her unpaid internship at Amnesty International

daughter of the people who own Ticketmaster

an aerobics instructor/ Fulbright scholar who donates all of her modeling money to Amnesty International and can get backstage passes to anything

WARNING!
Most Wanted:
She is known to be charming and dangerous

BREAKUP ✏ QUIZ #4

True or False:

T F

☐ ☐ I have considered going on a blind date with my aunt's mah-jong partner's nephew.

☐ ☐ I have conducted business in a Hallmark store and/or pharmacy without bursting into tears upon hearing a particular Muzak selection.

☐ ☐ The business I was conducting was the hasty, second-thought purchase of a "sorry it's late" birthday card.

☐ ☐ I have worn makeup to the Department of Motor Vehicles.

☐ ☐ The "ring check" has practically become a reflex.

☐ ☐ I have used at least one dorky line, e.g., "Come here often?" (in an elevator).

☐ ☐ I had to look at the telephone key pad to remember my ex's phone number.

☐ ☐ I have participated in at least one on-line hot tub.

☐ ☐ I actually cheated at the college name game just to have something to say to that guy.

If you answered "true" to five or more of these questions, move on to Chapter 5. If not, keep working the bubble wrap and try again soon.

THE CHANCE

MEETING
NUMBER FOUR

WHERE:
on street; decide to have coffee

APPROPRIATE BODY LANGUAGE:
hug (optional: awkward same-side face-bump)

APPROPRIATE THING TO SAY:
Hi…good to see you…not much, great, really good,
the usual…what about you, yup, same old…she's fine…
I think the Republicans may have gone too far…sure,
let's stay in touch…

CHAPTER FIVE:
A BREAKUP ALMANAC

This is the one almanac that knows better than to provide you with a long-term schedule of sunsets and full-moonlit nights. Instead, this handy reference tool puts a wealth of breakup information —history, linguistics, mythology—right at your fingertips, and allows you to find a meaningful place for your romantic ex-convergence within the big blue breakup cosmology.

*And remember, once you've made it this far,
new starts are always in the stars.*

*Congratulations on
turning the tides.*

A WORLD HISTORY OF THE BREAKUP

I t's no accident that every breakup feels like the end of an era. Breakups have existed and persisted since the dawn of time—and, in fact, they lie at the core of watershed events throughout history and prehistory. Use this timeline to trace the evolution of the breakup and to find a larger historical context for the fall of your romantic empire.

I.
The
Biggest
Bang

The forces of gravity
that brought hydrogen and helium
together are the same that,
when things get too hot and heavy,
will drive them apart.

A WORLD HISTORY OF THE BREAKUP

II. Early Geologic Ages

PRECAMBRIAN:

The continents, once close, begin to drift apart.

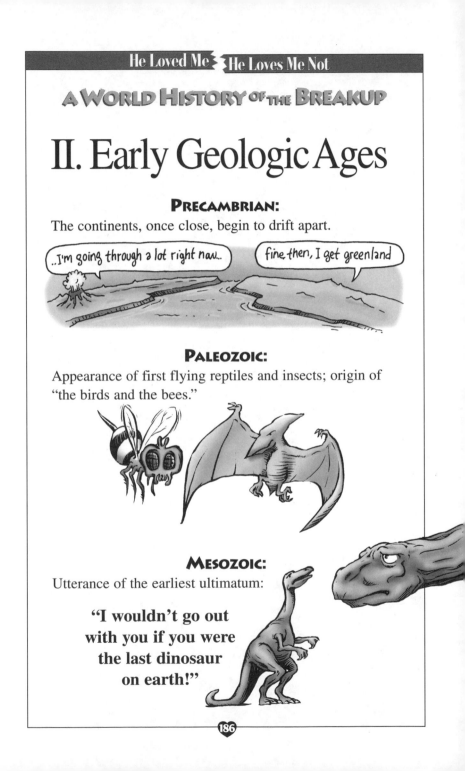

PALEOZOIC:

Appearance of first flying reptiles and insects; origin of "the birds and the bees."

MESOZOIC:

Utterance of the earliest ultimatum:

"I wouldn't go out with you if you were the last dinosaur on earth!"

A WORLD HISTORY OF THE BREAKUP

CENOZOIC:

Calcium carbonate shells of marine plants and animals create formations of chalk, prehistoric ancestor of Valentine candy.

ICE AGE AND GREAT FLOOD:

Only couples cruise known to end peacefully.

Happy now, Mr. We-Never-Get-Out-Anymore?

STONE AGE:

Time of decreased pressure on dating couples; that is, among largely nomadic peoples, the question of "settling down" was beside the point. Still, archaeological evidence points to an evolutionary insult commonly used by Neanderthal women: "He's *such* a *Cro-Magnon!*"

A WORLD HISTORY OF THE BREAKUP

111. The Ancient Near East

Breakup communication is revolutionized by invention of hieroglyphic writing in Egypt (c. 3100 B.C.E.), allowing not only for carving of "Dear Job" letters, but also for dramatic smashing of clay tablets upon receipt.

During the Age of the Prophets, a series of men come to fancy themselves as the earthly link to the divine (modern manifestation: "God's gift"). Their heavenly bidding often involved making their girlfriends serve as secular symbols of a theocratic manifest destiny. Talk about being *used*.

HOSEA AND GOMER:

At Yahweh's command, the prophet Hosea (8th C. B.C.E.) marries Gomer, a prostitute in the Baalistic cult. The divine intention: that Hosea's treatment of Gomer represent the fate of the Israelites if they don't shape up. Accordingly, Hosea generally gives Gomer the cold shoulder, eventually divorcing her, only to then buy her back for "fifteen shekels and a homer and lethech of barley."

A WORLD HISTORY OF THE BREAKUP

IV. CLASSICAL ANTIQUITY

CULTURED MEDITERRANEAN WOMEN STILL RUN THE RISK OF GETTING INVOLVED WITH ACTUAL 'PHILISTINES.'

With progress comes ambition. Men are no longer content merely acting as high-class escorts. Now, in order to both serve and impress the gods—and, one would surmise, the girls—they must found cities, capture thrones, build nations. Yet behind every one of these great men, it seems, are some really annoyed women.

DIDO AND AENEAS:

Dido, founder and queen of Carthage, falls hard for the irresistibly distant Aeneas, and hurls herself onto a pyre when she finds out that he's leaving her to found Rome (c. 1200 B.C.E.) Aeneas later marries Lavinia, the Sandra Dee of Virgil's time.

MEDEA AND JASON:

Medea loves Jason enough not only to put up with his Argonaut buddies, but also to help him score the Golden Fleece and secure the throne of Iolcus. But all that give, give, give isn't enough, apparently, to stop Jason from running around with Creusa, whom Medea knocks off with the deadly "gift" of a burning dress. (Important lesson for today's lovers: Lambskin—exciting, but unreliable.)

A WORLD HISTORY OF THE BREAKUP

V. THE ROMAN EMPIRE

EMPEROR CLAUDIUS (reigned 268-270 A.D.) calls for the execution of an irritating young man named **VALENTINE**. He has no idea that the martyr will go on to become the patron saint of Things That Were Never Meant to be Heart-Shaped and to lend his name to an annual festival of romance that fittingly falls during nature's bitterest, slushiest month.

As nations blend and expand into empires with ever-more complex and set-in-stone social orders, what begins to emerge are the Wuthering Heights, the My Fair Ladies, the West Side Stories of love that can't last.

JULIUS CAESAR AND COSSUTIA:

An ambitious young Caesar (102-44 B.C.E.) breaks off his engagement to Cossutia because she doesn't belong to the politically powerful equestrian class. Consequently, parents seeking power marriages for their daughters begin to think twice before discouraging their adolescent obsession with horses.

A WORLD HISTORY OF THE BREAKUP

VI. The Middle Ages

★ CHIVALRY NOT DEAD.

★ VOLUNTARY CELIBACY GAINS DRAMATICALLY IN POPULARITY.

Here, Let me get that.

The structure of society itself continues to doom many romances. The institutions of the day, when called into play during a breakup, also render minimal the rate of "getting back together."

ABELARD AND HELOISE:

Young Heloise (1101-1163) has what we can only assume was a sexually as well as intellectually satisfying affair with her tutor, the Parisian scholar Abelard. Once word gets out, though, Heloise's uncle has Abelard hunted down and castrated. At Abelard's request, Heloise takes vows at the local holy order. His suggestion is considered an early manifestation of the "If I can't have you, no one can" syndrome.

A WORLD HISTORY of the BREAKUP

VII. Renaissance and Reformation

> **PROGRESS:** Challenge to Ptolemaic theory that men are the center of the universe.
>
> **MITIGATING FACTOR:** Ensuing Copernican Revolution establishes self-absorbing notion that planetary system revolves around prime tanning hours.
>
> **ALSO,** advancement of Calvinist doctrine of "predestination" paves way for fatalistic secular breakup, i.e. "It just wasn't meant to be."

Chagrined to discover that the world does not revolve around them, men make extra sure to have other big strong guys (Parliament, the Pope) around to back them up.

HENRY VIII, CATHERINE, AND ANNE BOLEYN:

Henry VIII (1491-1547), who wants to dump his wife Catherine because she is too old to provide him an heir (probably just as well), becomes infatuated with lady-in-waiting Anne Boleyn (1505-1536). When his request for marital annulment runs into major red tape, he gets Parliament to grant him power roughly equivalent to the Pope's, and then goes ahead and grants himself the annulment. Later, when Anne also fails to beget a prince, Henry fabricates charges of treason and has her executed. (Modern single girls hoping to land an absolute monarch should pay heed: when he says "I want you to bear my children," he is *serious*.)

A WORLD HISTORY OF THE BREAKUP

VIII. The "New" World

The return of brave explorers from distant lands with exotic spices, luxury textiles, and precious gems leads to a temporary increase in the number of women who stay in relationships longer than they mean to.

IX. The American Revolution

Records of tavern gossip document the personal rebellion of one feisty female colonial who broke things off with a member of her local militia by tossing a mug of grog in his face and exclaiming: "No wonder they call you a *Minute*-Man!" This remark soon becomes known as "the parting shot heard 'round the world."

A WORLD HISTORY OF THE BREAKUP

X. Early-Modern Europe

DISAPPEARANCE OF BUBONIC PLAGUE IN WESTERN EUROPE (C. 1720) AND THUS OF MAJOR EXCUSE FOR DATE CANCELLATION AND/OR BREAKUP.

Though women still have few "ins" with Parliament and other official bodies of power, they are beginning to learn the importance of networking.

CATHERINE THE GREAT AND PETER.

Catherine (1762-1796) puts up with Peter's drinking, womanizing, and flying off the handle for only so long. Fortunately for her, he'd made quite a few other enemies—including some in the army, who help her plot a successful coup.

A WORLD HISTORY OF THE BREAKUP

XI. INDUSTRIAL REVOLUTION

Railway brings mixed news for romance.

GOOD: long-distance lovers no longer have to get the horse for the weekend in order to rendezvous.

BAD: singles on railway platform subjected to new, industrialized, form of lovey-dovey—that is, the forlorn, jogging-alongside-the-departing-train goodbye.

The advent of the telephone is not to revolutionize the breakup until later development of features such as call-screening, unlisted numbers, and "I can't talk, I'm on the other line." In the meantime, however, the circumstances of the telephone's invention do give rise at least to topical crank call used to harass exes:

Caller: "[Name], come quickly, I want you...*NOT!*"

A WORLD HISTORY OF THE BREAKUP

XII. Modern America

Two world wars, a depression, an arms race, an energy crisis, the information superhighway, the Menudo phenomenon—the modern factors influencing breakups in society as we now know them are far too numerous to explore individually. There remain, however, copious lessons to be learned from the role models of the day, particularly in the key areas that distinguish our nation from the pack:

Technology

WINONA RYDER AND JOHNNY DEPP:
Get tattoo of lover's name only if you're sure your artist has the skill to one day conceal lettering in illustration.

OLIVIA NEWTON-JOHN AND MATT LATTANZI:
Xanadu—it can't last.

Winona

A WORLD HISTORY OF THE BREAKUP

BUSINESS

DONALD TRUMP AND IVANA EX-TRUMP:

Say "I Will Survive" with your own line of omnipresent perfume.

LEE MAJORS AND FARRAH FAWCETT:

Do not break up with someone whose pin-up will come back to haunt you when the 1970s do.

ART

WOODY "HUSBANDS AND WIVES" ALLEN AND MIA FARROW:

Do not provoke the wrath of a major Hollywood screenwriter.

NORA "HEARTBURN" EPHRON AND CARL BERNSTEIN:

Become a major Hollywood screen writer.

A Breakup Book of

SAINTS

ou may not think of yourself as a religious person; in fact, a lousy breakup can easily bolster anyone's atheism. On the other hand, your suffering could also be taken as evidence that there is a God, and he/she is still wrathful about the time you blamed the turpentine incident on your little brother.

But no matter how devout you fancy yourself already, breakups do inspire little religious moments all their own, constant musings on the afterlife, the workings of fate, the body/spirit duality ("I am in **hell**;" "It wasn't **meant to be**;" "This frosting is **divine!**").

So while you're **praying** for the phone to ring or convincing yourself that never again will you know anyone **biblically**, you may as well get some saints on your side. Here are some whose specialties you may find particularly relevant, either to you or to those whose services you will come to depend on. Buy candles in bulk, and invoke away!

For issues of character and circumstance:

Anthony of Padua, to whom a votive candle is lit for the recovery of a lost, stolen, or confiscated article of personal value.

Afra, Margaret of Cortona, Thais, and Mary Magdalene, patronesses of fallen women

Catherine of Alexandria and **Catherine of Siena**, patronesses of spinsters

Christopher, patron saint of travelers (say, to Hell)

Christopher (another one), patron of bachelors (apparently never met the Catherines)

Francis Patrizi, patron of reconciliations. Obscure.

Jude, patron saint of lost causes

Mathurin, patron of fools

Rita, invoked against loneliness

Stanislav Kostka, invoked against doubt and palpitations

Uncumber, invoked against, well, men

Claire of Assisi, patroness, by 1958 decree of Pope Pius XII, of television

No, no, go back one..

For ailments, psychosomatic and otherwise:

Bibiana, patroness invoked against hangovers

Dymphna, invoked against sleepwalking

Emerentia, invoked against stomachache

Job, invoked against ulcers

Notker Bablulus, invoked against stammering

uh, hi ... you dropped this ...

NOTKER BABLULUS DON'T FAIL ME NOW!

For necessary goods and services:

Arnulph of Soissons, patron of bakers (he is always depicted holding what appears to be a pizza shovel). Also, Elizabeth of Hungary.

Augustine of Hippo, patron of brewers. But careful what you wish for; he is also responsible for the linking of sexual pleasure to "original sin" (he clearly had no idea about "beer goggles").

Crispin and Crispinian, patrons of shoemakers

Drogo, patron of coffeehouse owners

Macarius of Alexandria (the Younger), patron of pastry cooks

Martin de Porres, patron of hairdressers

And some we'd canonize if we could

St. Ambivalent, watcher-overer of those who will die if they spend another minute either with or without him

St. Carbo of Pepperidge, patron of comfort food

St. Henna, invoked against ill-conceived, impulsive hair mutations

St. Invective, patron of witty, biting remarks thought of at the moment of need

St. Maarten, St. John, St. Thomas, St. Kitts. Pray for your rich aunt to decide you "need to get away."

A <u>Nature</u> <u>Special:</u>
<u>Romance</u> <u>and</u> <u>Breakups</u>
<u>in</u> <u>the</u> <u>Animal</u> <u>Kingdom</u>

By Lynn Harris
Ivory Tower U.
Department of Zoology

Animals have shown us so many things about the world we live in: the strength and frailty of nature's delicate balance, the urgency of preservation, the body at the bottom of the ravine. They also teach us about ourselves and one another: how to live (either bring in food or have it delivered), how to love (indifferently, unless food is available), how to say goodbye (if person A does not provide food, proceed to person B). And imagine what we'd learn if—in the fulfillment of a heady fantasy that has gripped the human imagination since the beginning of our coexistence—animals could actually talk about mating and magnetism:

> "Mating for life is really the most wonderful thing
> that's ever happened to me—well, to us."

> "Forget it, sister, just clone your own."

"How do you expect me to meet anybody worthwhile when I've got this heinous bandanna tied around my neck?"

"Pigs are men."

But scientists and singles who seek to partake of the wild wisdom of our animal friends have, of course, no choice but to rely on pure and keen observation. Here is what Breakup Girl's fieldwork has revealed about the breakup habits of our fuzzy, finny, and feathered friends.

The pig

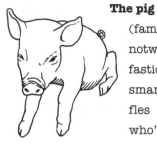

(family Suidae). Their reputations notwithstanding, pigs are clean and fastidious. They are cute, pink, and smart; they can sniff out rare truffles under six inches of soil. So who's insulting whom?

The young dog, or puppy

(canis lupus ambivalensus). The origin and meaning of the term puppy love leaves little room for argument. Puppy behavior may be broken down into three steps:

1. "I love love love you I can hardly stand how much I love you you are positively the most exciting other being I have ever experienced I can't even bear it and I will run and get that ball for you no matter how many times or how far you throw it or even if you throw it into the mud, well especially if you throw it into the mud and I want to lick your face and—"

2. Fall asleep.

3. Repeat cycle, addressing yourself to the first person you see when you wake up.

Important note: Despite its traditional attribution to puppies, this behavioral pattern appears to remain constant throughout what one might otherwise presume to be maturity.

The African freshwater snail

(bulinus truncatus). These savvy gastropods change their sexual practices depending on the water temperature in their habitat. In cold water, the snails self-fertilize; only when it's warm do they bother with intercourse. Needless to say, natural selection has not favored male snails who use the line "Baby, it's cold outside."

The guppy

(poecilia reticulata). Scientists claim that a male guppy will actually seek out geekier, less popular guppies to swim around with so that he will look more attractive by comparison. Among humans, this technique was adopted and made famous by The Fonz (Arthur Fonzarelli).

The fish

(superclass Pisces). Some types have huge, bulging eyes. Human corollary: people who wear their hair big so that their butts will look smaller.

The caterpillar

Some species actually carry permanent wound-like growths. This is a defense mechanism with which we may take great, if not obvious, metaphorical liberties—as if to tell a new predator, "Don't bother," or, as Vladimir Nabokov has put it, "Don't eat me—I have already been squashed, sampled, and rejected."

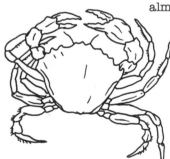

The arrowhead crab

(brachyura decapoda). These perspicacious crustaceans have eyes set so far apart that they can see almost a complete circle. They have thus evolved with the power of nearly 20/20 hindsight; when breakups occur, they routinely smack themselves on the head with their pincers, as if to say, "I should have seen it coming."

The parrot

(order Psittaciformes). She knows what she wants.

The owl

(order Strigiformes). Owls have remarkably sharp ears, making it impossible for them to claim to a mate that they "didn't hear" something. They are, on the other hand, entirely colorblind. There is thus no basis in owl society for relationships to founder for reasons such as "No, this sweater is mauve and this one is puce! How can you not tell the difference?!"

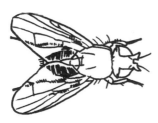

The fruit fly

(Drosophila bifurca). Scientists recently discovered that one Southwestern and Central American species of fruit fly produces sperm 20 times longer than its own body—that's 1,000 times longer than human sperm. Are we supposed to be impressed?

The mosquito

(culicidae). Relatively brief life span gives rise to increased pressure on young mosquitoes to settle down and reproduce, as in:

—When are you going to give me some beautiful grandchildren?

—Tomorrow, Ma, relax!

The Pacific salmon

(family Salmonidae). Each year these salmon swim upstream to their parents' house, indicating that in-law relations are complex and binding.

The rodent, various types

(order Rodentia). Couples split up immediately after mating, a pattern that has led some scientists to speculate that when it comes to what they have to tell us about human behavior, experiments with mazes and eyeliners may be beside the point.

Central American frog

(Physalaemus). The male sings to attract mates, but in doing so risks attracting frog-eating bats. Female frogs generally feel pretty fortunate about this, having heard that most human males would sooner be eaten by bats than arrange something nice like a serenade.

The bat

(order Chiroptera). Bats determine how close they are to something (or someone) by bouncing sound off it and seeing how long it takes to come back. When they say, "I'm getting a weird vibe from you—you've been distant," they are always right.

The butterfly

(family Danidae). The male travels from flower to flower, mixing and carrying scents on his hind legs until he has created the perfect perfume for his intended. Unfortunately, by that time he's usually late.

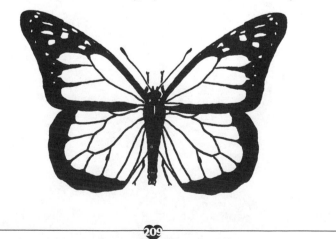

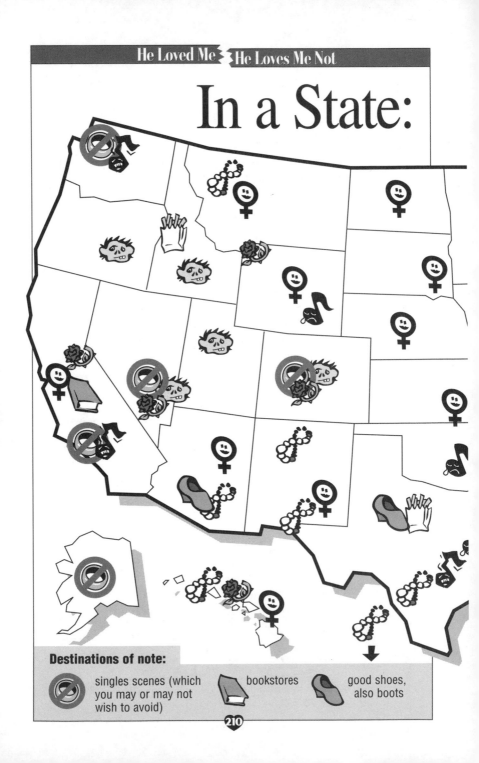

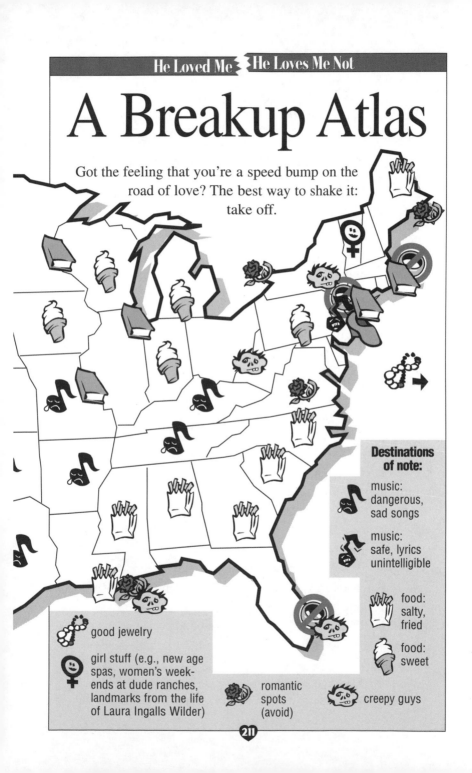

A Breakup Atlas

Got the feeling that you're a speed bump on the road of love? The best way to shake it: take off.

Destinations of note:

music: dangerous, sad songs

music: safe, lyrics unintelligible

food: salty, fried

food: sweet

good jewelry

girl stuff (e.g., new age spas, women's weekends at dude ranches, landmarks from the life of Laura Ingalls Wilder)

romantic spots (avoid)

creepy guys

A Breakup for All Seasons

During a relationship,
you run your life on a calendar all your own.
Let's say, for example, that you guys got together on January 20. What would otherwise have been "May 23," you will now think of as *Brian 4, 3* (4 months, 3 days). What would have been "September 11" will be *3 SDLUHB* (3 Shopping Days Left Until His Birthday).

But now that you're back on the standard Gregorian calendar, you might flip ahead and find it pretty much blank, except for the day you're getting your period (and you can be fairly sure that you're getting it). Well, there may be more special days there than meet the eye. We've talked you through Valentine's Day; here's a special review of some of the other feasts and festivals that may surround your hell-day:

New Year's Day, January 1. On this day in Roman times, sacrifices were made to Janus, the *two-faced god*. Buy yourself some bubbly; you've sacrificed enough.

Groundhog Day, February 2. If your spies see him with a 5 o'clock shadow, he has six more weeks of bumming.

Lincoln's Birthday, February 12. But other than *that*, Mrs. Lincoln, how was the relationship?

Washington's Birthday, February 22. *Sales.*

Shrove Tuesday, February 28. Also known as Fat Tuesday or Pancake Tuesday. *Psych.*

Saint Patrick's Day, March 17. Celebrate with Sean Connery movie marathon.

April Fool's Day, April 1. "Your fly's unzipped."

Arbor Day, April 28. Save a tree—use his cute little notes as "scrap."

Mother's Day, second Sunday in May. Do not watch TV the week before unless you don't mind sparking your biological tinderbox. (Of course, watching anything with Kathie Lee Gifford and Cody will put that spark right out.)

Memorial Day, May 29. Start planning around Groundhog Day to make sure you have a barbeque to go to.

Flag Day, June 14. Take some time to reflect on all the red flags you should have noticed.

Father's Day, third Sunday in June. See Mother's Day.

Independence Day, July 4. Call him to tell him you're getting along just fine without him. Call him to make sure he got the message. Leave a stickie on his door (plus some red, white, and blue cupcakes) reminding him to listen to his machine.

Labor Day, September 4. Marks official end of summer romance.

Columbus Day, October 12. *Sales.*

Election Day, November 7.

Halloween, October 31. Talk about your breakup with the kids who come to your door until they're afraid to take your candy.

Exercise your right to vote. Write yourself in, thinking, "'More space,' huh? Now what if you were married to the *President*, then you'd have some 'space,' now wouldn't you? Well, citizen, you've lost your chance...!"

Thanksgiving, fourth Thursday in November. Your relatives' official holiday motto: "Won't your *friend* be joining us this year?"

Christmas, December 25. Your married friends spread Yuletide cheer with family-and-golden-retriever-photograph cards and envelopes embossed with their non-cumbersome hyphenated names. Your single —"and lovin' it"—friends weigh in with postcards from the tropics ("Here I am in Cancun, with my beautiful cabana boy Lorenzo!")

A Breakup for All Seasons

Other observances you may
or may not wish to take part in:

January:
National Hot Tea Month
National Soup Month
Oatmeal Month
21: National Hugging Day*
23: National Pie Day

February
Creative Romance Month*
National Weddings Month*
National Snack Food Month
7: National Hangover
   Awareness Day
weekend before Valentine's
   Day: Chocolate Festival,
Norman, OK
13: Clean Out Your
   Computer Day (purge or
   save on floppy all sexually
   explicit e-mails exchanged)

March
National Noodle Month
19-25 American Chocolate
   Week

April
National Anxiety Month
National Welding Month (see
   "What to Do with His
   Stuff," p. 45)
National Woodworking
Month (ditto)
7: No Housework Day (as if)
third week: National Lingerie
   Week
30: National Honesty Day*

May
National High Blood
   Pressure Education Month
   (lessons: avoid relationships; avoid not having
   relationships)
National Salad Month*
first Thursday: National Day
   of Prayer (observe yourself
   or let others, such as your
   not normally religious
   mother, do it for you)
second week: National Self-
   Help Book Week

* plan on staying home

June

National Frozen Yogurt
   Month (but save room for
   July)
Thursday after Memorial
   Day: Soap Opera Fan Fair
   (Mackinaw City, MI)
first Saturday: World's
   Largest Garage Sale (South
   Bend, IN)
first full week: National
   Fragrance Week*

July

National Ice Cream Month
   (but save room for
   October)
1: Anniversary of debut of
   Court TV (potentially
   day-long observance)
3: Compliment-Your-Mirror
   Day*
4: National Country Music
   Day
12: Video Games Day

August

6: Friendship Day*
week of first Monday:
   National Smile Week*
15: National Relaxation Day
18: Bad Poetry Day
25: Kiss-And-Make-Up Day*

September

5: Be Late for Something
   Day (enjoy—you've got an
   excuse that no one will tri-
   fle with)
10: National Grandparents
   Day (do not call home
   unless you don't mind
   answering questions about
   when your parents will be
   able to celebrate this day)
third week: National Singles
   Week*

October

National Dessert Month
National Pasta Month
National Pizza Month
National Popcorn Month

November

Jewelry Month
19: Have a Bad Day Day
24: Sinkie Day (honoring
   people who occasionally
   dine over the kitchen sink.
   For real.)

December

21: Humbug Day
26: National Whiner's Day

Romance and Breakup Patterns in Humans: Through the Life Cycle

phase	romance	breakup
Preschool	He's daddy when playing House	He's the dog
K–4	————[N/A due to cooties]————	
5–Jr. High	Tell everyone you like him	Tell everyone you hate him
High School	Go to mall	Go to the other mall
College	Sleep together when drunk	Sleep together when drunk
Real Life	He's daddy when playing House	He's the dog

"IF IT'S 'NOT ME,' THEN DUMP SOMEONE ELSE!"

Top Ten Breakup Myths

It's not you.

Roses, schmozes.

"The love you take is equal to the love you make."

All women always want commitment.

I never realized how much I enjoy spending time alone.

Now I'll have so much more time to exercise.

Now *that's* one thing I *won't* miss.

Sure, I'll return the sweats.

I think it would be healthy for him to start dating again.

I'm really happy for them.

THE CHANCE
MEETING
NUMBER FIVE

WHERE:
suburban supermarket

APPROPRIATE BODY LANGUAGE:
that two-step you do when you're
trying to get by someone and you both
keep going to the same side

APPROPRIATE THING TO SAY:
1. "Excuse me."
-pause-
2. "Did we used to date?"

INDEX

Hydroxy Humectant Liposome Collagen Système, 156
Switzerland, 43, 47
swooning, *see* fainting

T

talk shows, 27
  also see Rolonda
tatoos, 149
Taylor, Elizabeth, 25
Taylor, James, 35
toothbrush, 38, 43, 173
Thelma and Louise, 35, 117
trophy date, 41
Trump, Donald and Ivana, 197
turf wars, 46
Two Braised Ducks with Onion and Broccoli Purees, Caramel Vinegar Sauce, and Croutons, 96

U

Nothing for "U." Figures.

V

Valentine's Day
  blooper, 15
  candy, 187
  dealing with, 104
  origin of, 190
Van Dyke, Dick, 44
Victoria's Secret, 35
voodoo doll, 39, 118

W

warning signs, 172-174
weddings

as place to meet people, 144
as site of chance meeting, 153
etiquette for the single girl, 142
other people's, 140-143
West, Mae, 117
Who Framed Roger Rabbit?, 168
Woolery, Chuck, 27
workplace, breakups in the, 86
World Wide Web, 40

X

X-Files, The, 163

Y

Yeast-Gard, 177
"Y.M.C.A.," 132

Z

Ziggy, 83

ABOUT THE CREATORS

LYNN HARRIS is co-author, with ex-boyfriend Larry Berger, of the deliciously funny *Tray Gourmet: Be Your Own Chef in the College Cafeteria* (Lake Isle Press). She is the humor columnist for *Brooklyn Woman* magazine. Her articles have also been published in *Glamour, Ladies' Home Journal, Mademoiselle, Working Woman, Parade, Seventeen,* and many others. She performs stand-up comedy and cabaret theatre in New York City, and plays on women's ice and roller hockey teams. She graduated from Yale University.

Lynn has three major breakups to her credit.

CHRIS KALB designed and illustrated *Tray Gourmet: Be Your Own Chef in the College Cafeteria* (Lake Isle Press), as well as *The On-Track Trainer* (Cornell Hotel School). He has also illustrated *Up Your* [S.A.T.] *Score* (Workman) and *'Scuse Me While I Kiss This Guy* (Fireside).

Chris is art director for *Derivatives Strategy* magazine and the *Science Fiction Weekly* Web page.

Chris' comic strip in *The Yale Daily News* won him Scripps-Howard's Charles M. Schulz Award for the nation's most promising college cartoonist.

Chris has always been the dumpee.

DENISE WINTERS

DANIEL P. CREIGHTON